11080

# SAILING WITH
# MR BELLOC

# SAILING WITH
# MR BELLOC

DERMOD MacCARTHY

COLLINS HARVILL
8 Grafton Street, London W1
1986

William Collins Sons and Co Ltd
London · Glasgow · Sydney · Auckland
Toronto · Johannesburg

BRITISH LIBRARY CATALOGUING IN PUBLICATION DATA
MacCarthy, Dermod
Sailing with Mr Belloc.
1. Belloc, Hilaire  2. Yachts and yachting
– Great Britain
I. Title
797.1'24'0924      GV814

ISBN 0-00-272775-7

First published by Collins Harvill 1986
© Dermod MacCarthy 1986

Typeset by Rowland Phototypesetting Ltd
Bury St Edmunds, Suffolk
Printed and bound in Great Britain by
Robert Hartnoll Ltd,
Bodmin, Cornwall

TO
FRANCES PHIPPS

# ACKNOWLEDGEMENTS

I AM particularly grateful to Mr Frank G. G. Carr CB, CBE, Chairman of The World Ship Trust, for starting me on the search for the origins of Belloc's pilot cutter and for his frank, useful and kind advice. I am also grateful to Mr J. H. Arrowsmith, Assistant to the Registrar of British Ships, Port of Jersey, for his records of the 'Yacht' from 1846 onwards; to Mr M. R. Bullen and Mr B. E. Ching, Deputy Harbour Masters, St Helier, for records of the Marine Marchande de Jersey and for discovering the article in the Annual Bulletin of the Société Jersiaise 1966, which is quoted on pages 27–8; and to Miss K. Langrish in the Information Office of Lloyd's Register of Shipping.

For their help and criticism over sailing matters, I wish to thank Dr Douglas Gairdner, Editor of the *Cruising Association Bulletin*, Mr Denis Harward, Vice-President of Exeter Maritime Museum, Dr Trevor Mann, a Watch Officer of SS *Winston Churchill*, and Mr Francis Warre Cornish MA. I should also like to thank two authorities on Hilaire Belloc, Mr A. N. Wilson and Mrs Clare Sheppard, whose comments I value very much, and Mr Charles Eustace, great-grandson of Belloc, for a day revisiting King's Land.

Grateful acknowledgement is made to A. D. Peters & Co Ltd for permission, on behalf of Hilaire Belloc's Estate, to quote passages from his letters and published works, and to the Controller HM Stationery Office and the Hydrographer of the Navy for permission to quote from the *Channel Pilot*.

Concerning the illustrations, I wish to acknowledge the contribution that the late J. J. Hall's photographs make to this book. Jim Hall died in 1959. He sailed many times on the *Jersey*. His camera was a small box Brownie to which he occasionally added a little portrait lens. Mr Belloc liked being photographed, there is no doubt about that, but hardly ever posed; in most of Jim's snapshots he was caught unawares.

For permission to reproduce photographs, I am grateful to Lady Phipps, Mrs Peter Belloc, Mr Matthew Jebb and Mrs Kitty Roughead. Some pictures I took myself with an Ensign box camera.

# CONTENTS

# ILLUSTRATIONS

*Between pages 112 and 113*
Jim Hall steering and feeling low
At the helm
Mr Belloc on the beach at Sandgate
Barges at Pin Mill
Discovering the ways of the sea in 1929
With a fair wind

*Between pages 144 and 145*
In Ostend
Middelburg, on the Veere Canal
Approaching Harwich
The Chapman Light in the Lower Thames
In pensive mood
The deck of the *Jersey*
The *Jersey* at Hole Haven
Hilaire Belloc aged 79

# INTRODUCTION

HILAIRE Belloc was half French. He was a Catholic, a European, a historian, a disillusioned politician, a traveller, a poet and a 'yachtsman', though the image that that word usually conjures up does not fit him. His humour, which is famous, was intensely ironical. Perhaps it stemmed from an inner sadness or fatalism, but it was not bitter. It was refreshing and converted into laughter the grimmer sides of life. He also loved invective and was a master of it. He could use it splendidly in defence of a cause or to destroy an adversary or a fool; but also, of course, simply for fun, and chance annoyances or predicaments in harbours were often the occasion for it.

When I first went sailing with him I knew practically nothing about his past life, his books or his highly controversial views on many things. I was unaware that although to many people he was a great man, to some he was intolerable, a bigot and a boor. I knew he was a powerful defender of the Roman Catholic faith, but as I had been scared of Catholic churches as a child, this feature of him made his formidable personality additionally alarming to me. I did know, however, that my father was a lifelong friend of his and loved his company. (I was also to discover later, on reading my father's literary criticism, that he had championed Belloc as an author all his life.)

When I met Hilaire Belloc in 1931 I was in my early twenties and naturally I always called him 'Mr Belloc' or 'Sir'. In those days the older generation were not called by their Christian names by the younger, unless they were old family friends. Those who were relations were called 'Uncle' . . . or 'Aunt' . . . or sometimes 'Cousin so and so'. Hence the title of these memoirs, which expresses a relationship, one of respect. It does not convey the admiration and affection which I hope will be apparent in the story.

Although Belloc died more than thirty years ago now, there are still quite a lot of people alive who knew him, for he had a vast number of friends. And there are many who, though they would not say that they knew him, did meet him or encounter him and therefore felt his impact. With these people in mind when writing this account, it was easy to launch into a description of his sailing days without having to explain him; for the imprint of his extraordinary character cannot have faded. But for others who never met him and who may have read very little of his history, biographies, travel books, poetry, satirical verse or even his essays on the sea and sailing, some explanation of him is necessary, for he was a phenomenon. For those who want to know more about him and his significance as a twentieth-century personality – in fact, an Edwardian character who lived on – a short biographical sketch is given as an appendix to this book.

What was he like to meet in those days? Well, whether it was as a distinguished, cloaked figure in the Reform Club, or as an 'old sea dog' aboard his pilot cutter, in a seaman's jersey shiny with age, unshaven and bleary eyed from the salt winds, and with 'Old Bill' trousers containing his belly like an egg cup with braces, Belloc's appearance was always extraordinary, formidable and fascinating to contemplate.

He was a man who did not look you in the face very often. His eyes met yours very briefly, but when they did it was startling to find how blue they were; a blueness all the more striking because of the blackness of his clothes and the redness of his face.

He was no longer, now that he was in his sixties, the bold

mariner or tough old skipper that his appearance suggested. From his past experiences and escapades he had developed a great respect for the dangers that lurked behind the temporarily benign face of the sea or sky and his spirits noticeably fell when their mood became ugly; knowing that if things got bad he could no longer summon up the strength required to work a ship or simply to hold on, and must depend on his young friends, most of whom were very inexperienced. But stamina he still had.

As for the sailing – that irresistible appeal the sea has for some men was the same then as it is now. Such differences as there were are explained in the chapter 'The Way We Sailed Then'. But the boat Belloc sailed, which was the last he was to own, was a remarkably special one, even in the 1930s, and would be nigh impossible to come upon today. Two pilot cutters were well known at the time, *Jolie Brise*, built in 1913, described by Robin Bryer, well cared for and still sailing today[1]; and *Cariad*, Frank Carr's Bristol Channel pilot cutter, built in 1904, now in the Maritime Museum at Exeter. Both were much younger vessels than Belloc's *Jersey*. These memoirs are therefore written also as a portrait of his ancient boat.

[1] In *Jolie Brise: A Tall Ship's Tale* (Secker & Warburg: London, 1982).

# A NOTE ON
# HILAIRE BELLOC'S VOICE

WHENEVER Mr Belloc's remarks are quoted in the pages that follow, the reader must hear them spoken with the *r* pronounced in the French way; that is, in the back of the mouth between the tongue and the soft palate. It is true that French people of the south vibrate the tip of the tongue like the Italians and the Burgundians roll the *r* loudly somewhere in the front of the mouth, and the 'Parigots', the Parisian equivalent of London Cockneys, produce it from far back with the uvula; but the typical Frenchman speaks the *r* with his soft palate and yet it is not guttural like German or Dutch. In the text the letter *r* is printed in italics when Mr Belloc is quoted, as a reminder to hear it as he spoke it. His French *r*s were a strong part of his personality.

His voice, which expressed so much of his character, had two main qualities. It was musical and ringing when he spoke loudly, and husky yet still musical when he spoke softly. The sound of his voice then seemed to be in his breath, rather than in the vocal chords, particularly as he gently sang, which he did so much of the time while at sea, in a high-pitched, beautifully controlled, soft tenor. But the bell-like quality came into it as he spoke louder, sang louder, or laughed.

# HILAIRE BELLOC'S
# RETURN TO THE SEA

AT the beginning of the 1930s there was talk among some of Hilaire Belloc's friends about presenting him with a boat so that he could once again enjoy one of the things he had most enjoyed in life – sailing the sea. His previous boat, the *Nona*, had ended her days in 1927. She had sprung a bad leak and Hilaire Belloc only just managed to get her into harbour without sinking off the Norman coast. She was too old to go on. He finished her off with hammer and wedge, so that she was demolished and submerged, rather than left lying as an abandoned hulk. But if he had another boat he could once again go out 'on the salt', to the sea, which he says in *The Cruise of the Nona* 'has given me relief from men'.

Those who were interested in this idea were Frances Phipps, the chief contributor, Mary Herbert, Elizabeth Herbert, Duff Cooper and possibly others unrecorded.[1] The boat he thus acquired was a very old Channel Island pilot cutter. Her name was the *Jersey* and he found her in one of the creeks of Chichester Harbour. An undated letter from Tetton House, Somerset, to Mary Herbert contains the following:

---

[1] Lady Phipps, wife of the Ambassador Sir Eric Phipps; the Hon. Mrs Aubrey Herbert, Pixton Park, Dulverton, Somerset; the Hon. Mrs Mervyn Herbert, Tetton House, Somerset; the Right Honourable Duff Cooper, later Viscount Norwich.

I go to see both boats next week. One on Tuesday, the other on Saturday, 21st. I keep both on a string and when I've thoroughly worked it out I'll decide. It's an equal sum to be spent, but, in either case, as I said, the [thing] which I can only decide when I've seen the second one – is whether it's better to buy a hulk and spend the balance on refitting or to buy a partly fitted one which I have known for some weeks and which costs more but will need less doing to. I shall go by which looks the better *sea* boat. For that is everything: how they hold the sea. The *Nona* was perfect at it.

On 9 April 1931 he wrote from King's Land (his home) to Mary Herbert:

The wretched fiend of a typewriting woman in London addressed this to Pixton without asking *me*. I told her the right address, but as she'd written to Pixton in the past she thought she was right. The top copy will reach you in due time I suppose.

The famous Hulk was got off the mud on Monday, 6th, and towed to Itchenor 4 miles away where she shall be put in hand. The first thing is to paint her a fine shining black. Then to put sails on her, I'll take a photograph and send it you. I do hope the fools at Itchenor will do the work promptly. I have no trust in them or in any craftsmen in Sussex since the war. They hate work. So do I. It's good to be drinking again [he always gave up wine in Lent].

He wrote again on 12 April, giving this progress report:

I went to see the old boat yesterday. She is only a hulk, but the fitting up has begun. I have had her brought down to the moorings and hard in Chichester Harbour, where they will clean her, paint her, and put in the new spars that are needed and the new suit of sails, and I guess she ought to be ready to go out by the end of May. She has a fine big solid hull of oak, copper sheathed and she looks as though she would stand the sea very well. I still have about half the money in hand for the fitting up, it will probably cost a little more but that I can pay for myself. *I think it will be good to have some frills which make the boat habitable when one has people on board.* Then there is a proper chain and anchor to be got, her present anchor is insufficient and her chain is rusty and of all shapes and sizes, but chains and anchors are fairly cheap things. A more than sufficient length of chain and a proper anchor could be got for £12 or so.[1]

After the first proper 'sea trial' he wrote:

My dear Mary,
    I've just got back from the boat after bad weather. We could only get out on one day, Wednesday, and then, in the later part of the day, the wind rose very high and a dangerous sea with it, off the Anvil Point near St Alban's Head. We got out through the skill of Dermod MacCarthy, who is really excellent! He knows exactly what to do and has an exceptional 'eye' for distance and opportunity, which is everything at sea. I was only a passenger, but I vastly enjoyed it, in spite of fatigue.
    She is an *excellent* sea boat, I'm glad to say! Now that she has her new sails and properly balanced she is first rate: quite as good as the *Nona* in a sea way and handy, though heavy. She needs 3 younger men with me. I had 4. Peter Belloc, Atkin and Dermod, with A. D. Peters, who (the last) had not been to sea before. She can take six on board without crowding and 5 quite comfortably.
    The total cost to date is 287 odd leaving about 78 to 79 pounds for what will still have to be done: for though I was able to get out in rough weather she must be a good deal amenagée, and that will be for the winter when the yard has plenty of time. A block – or rather 2 blocks – gave way in the strain: luckily not vital ones. I blew up the man Shutler for not testing them.
    Before I go out again, which I hope to do this Summer, and with better luck of weather, I will have everything thoroughly tested and put into perfect order for the moment and new strong rigging when it is wanted, leaving the winter work for fittings and a proper companion and lighting and washing place. I don't think I shall have to spend more than £50 of my own money on her. She is a most delightful possession! You will be surprised when you see her for she is but an old and rough fishing boat – but so strong and good at her job: though aged. I guess about 40 years old.[2]

[1] As to the 'frills', so-called (the italics are mine), see Commander Bowles' views on washing, page 45.
[2] In fact we now know that the *Jersey* was built in 1846. See page 26.

I was, of course, extremely proud to have earned this 'oak leaf' on my first sail in the *Jersey*.

In that last letter is the first and only reference to the cost of the boat. The purchase price and the cost of the work to be done on her adds up to £366. It is very difficult to translate this into a comparable figure at today's prices. An oldish boat, say thirty years old and sound, 38 feet overall and of 19 tons gross displacement, if made of fibreglass and not suffering from 'osmosis', would probably cost about £9,000, perhaps less. If made of wood and really sound, a lot more.

Mr Frank Carr, owner of the pilot cutter *Cariad*, whose opinion I sought on this point, suggested that a reasonable comparison might be made with the purchase today of an unconverted east coast smack, which could be bought for between £3,000 and £4,000 and, when converted and brought up to yacht standards, might fetch £6,000. If Hilaire Belloc were alive today, an equivalent to the *Jersey* would certainly cost that much; it would have to be built of wood, fibreglass would be unthinkable. It was a handsome gift. He loved the boat and it suited his kind of sailing admirably.

The 'new' sails he refers to were in fact used Brixham trawler sails, given to him by Mr H. R. S. F. de V. Somerset (Bobby Somerset, former owner of the famous ocean-racing pilot cutter *Jolie Brise*). By luck they fitted very well.

The Herbert family and probably my father suggested to Belloc that he should take me on as one of his crew; and so it came about that I had the enormous enjoyment of sailing with the great man in the years between 1931 and 1938. During some of this time I also had the pleasure of looking after the *Jersey* to a great extent and sometimes sailing her with my own friends. That is all fifty years ago now. I am the only person left who was with him on those cruises and I feel compelled to attempt, before it is too late, some description of him and the way we sailed then.

# THE WAY WE SAILED THEN

THOSE whose sailing experience has been gained in the last thirty years or so, in yachts made of fibreglass, of improved design, rig and safety, may wonder at the haphazard way some amateurs went to sea in small boats between the two world wars. It did not require much in the way of equipment or money to get about Britain's coasts and beyond in reasonable safety and with vast enjoyment. There were always those who could make themselves more comfortable and a bit safer at sea because they were rich; but they did not enjoy sailing any more than those who were not – how could they? Hilaire Belloc was an old-fashioned 'ramshackle' sailor, who in his middle age pottered about the sea, as people would now say, in his ramshackle old boat; but how he enjoyed it!

Enterprising amateur sailors have existed from the mid-nineteenth century onwards, when Richard McMullen demonstrated that a gentleman was capable of sailing a yacht without a paid crew and moreover that it was quite respectable for him to do so. These exceptionally efficient, enterprising and bold yachtsmen became known because they wrote. Those who did not write remain unknown, but there are always a number of them among us in the sailing world today, as of yesterday. Hilaire Belloc was not a very skilled yachtsman, but is known as a sailor because he could write remarkably about the sea. His sailing may have been haphazard or rash (it is hard to tell sometimes from *The Cruise of the Nona*, which is no log book); but what puts him in the company of notable sailors of the past is his gift of description and his ability to transmit to us the effect of the sea on his powerful imagination.

The feats of yachtsmen today, racing round Britain, across the Atlantic or round the world, often alone, men or women, have made sailing a spectacle for the public beside which coastal cruising purely for pleasure seems a sleepy and uninteresting affair. Well, let it remain so; there are plenty of people who want no more than that. These memoirs belong to the days when boats were made of wood, their masts and spars also, their sails of canvas, their ropes of hemp; the days when amateurs explored the coasts happily and at greater leisure, with more room to anchor, with auxiliary motors that were less powerful and therefore less often used and which often would not start (Mr Belloc, of course, never had such a thing in his life); the days when the pleasures of sailing came from that sense of discovery one felt on entering any new harbour, however short the distance sailed to reach it. It was these things that Hilaire Belloc wanted to return to in his sixties; to revisit harbours and retrace passages he had made in the past was all he demanded. He was not interested in breaking new ground, indeed he would have had to go quite far to do so, but in tasting again the joys of familiarity with the sea; its headlands, tide rips, colours and moods. I think also in gratifying that innate deep conservatism of his, as he contemplated the boundaries of the sea with its shores and harbours, so permanent yet subtly changing in the lifetime of a man – a tempo of change he felt was more natural to man than the hurry and bustle already beginning in the 1930s.

# A CHILDHOOD MEMORY

M Y earliest memories of Mr Belloc belong to my sixth year. It
was then the middle of the war (the First World War) and I
was at Littlehampton on the Sussex coast in one of those houses
along the sea front – they are still there – which my father and
mother had been lent, I think in order that they might get their
children out of London to escape the bombs. An air raid in the
1914–18 war was a minute affair compared to those of the
Second World War, but the same fear hung over us all.

Mr Belloc's home was at King's Land near Horsham, twenty
miles inland, and the harbours of Shoreham and Littlehampton
were home ports to him. It was at Littlehampton that he once
took my mother sailing in the *Nona*, and, running aground some
way off the beach, had waded ashore with her in his arms and his
coat-tails floating on the water. The news that Mr Belloc was
coming seemed to put all the grown-ups into a state of agitation.
When was he arriving? Nobody knew. Suddenly he appeared.
There were a lot of other men with him. He was dressed in black.
He blew in, talked loudly, laughed and then disappeared in the
huge car that he had come in. At that time his paper *Land and
Water* was making a lot of money, he was 'rich', but it only lasted
a few years more. Suddenly he was back again. The huge car was
outside, the house was again full of men with their deep voices,

laughter and noise, and my father was among them. They crowded into the upstairs room, taking me with them. I was frightened by Mr Belloc and all his followers, and yet they seemed very benign and they were continually laughing about something. I was bewildered. He had brought some presents for the household – I can't remember what they were. I sat next to him and he suddenly produced a gigantic pocket-knife of the sort boys gaze at longingly in shop windows or can only dream of, but it was much much bigger. It had an incredible number of blades, corkscrews, gimlets, scissors and other gadgets and it was of shining steel and very heavy. He handed it to me and I knew that everyone was looking at me to see the effect of such a marvel on a little boy. 'There, Dermod, what do you think of *that!*' someone said. Mr Belloc had arrived with so many presents for the household that I suddenly took it into my head that he was giving this prodigious knife to me and I rather faintly said the words 'Oh, thank you'. There was a slight hush. Mr Belloc, or it may have been someone else, very gently took the knife back and I blushed with embarrassment. Then the buzz of voices filled the room again and the incident was over, except for the teasing that I knew was to come.

During the next fifteen years I do not think I met him or I would certainly have remembered it. But I had known his verses for bad children, which in earlier years one took with a certain awe, the enjoyment of the satire coming much later, and he often appeared in photographs or caricatures in the press with his black clothes and cloak, so I knew something of what to expect.

F. J. Sheed in 'Belloc the Apologist', in the *Tablet*, 1953, said 'you could no more ignore him than you could a tiger on your doorstep'. Well, one day in June 1931 I was asked by my mother to be at home in the afternoon because Mr Belloc wished to see me and talk about some sailing plans; to have a look at me, in fact, and ask about my sailing experience. I was a medical student by then, and left the dissecting room at St Bartholomew's Hospital early so as to get home in good time, and sure enough at about three o'clock a taxi arrived at 25 Wellington Square and the next minute 'the tiger' was ringing the front door bell. When he was shown in and I met him again, although I was now aged twenty I still had the childhood scene of Littlehampton in my memory; that of an alarming person, but one whom somehow I need not be afraid of because he was kind.

He filled with his black bulk the small dining-room where we sat down. He greeted my mother with great warmth and courtesy. I was introduced. He took me in at a glance. 'How are you my dear?' I felt the kindness. I loved him immediately, though still overawed, rather as if a large tiger had just spoken those words.

My father came down from his study at the top of the house and so much talk and laughter followed for the next hour that Mr Belloc seemed to have forgotten the purpose of his visit. Eventually he came round to it. I told him I shared a boat with another medical student. It was only 19 feet long, but seaworthy, an Aldeburgh sprat boat with a small cabin put on. We had got to know the ways of the sea on the east coast and had even been over to Flushing. Mr Belloc ended by giving me instructions to join him in the *Jersey*, on a date in July, at Poole where she was being fitted out for a summer cruise. He planned to sail westward.

# THE HISTORY OF
# THE *JERSEY*

I DO not know how Hilaire Belloc set about tracing the origins of his boat, which he acquired in 1931. He registered her under the name *Jersey* in Lloyd's Register of Yachts in 1934 and the entry ran as follows:

| Number | Name of yacht | Rig | Tonnage | Dimensions | |
|---|---|---|---|---|---|
| Consecutive | Jersey | Cutter | Official | length, | |
| 2815 | | | 12.98 | over all | 38ft |
| Official | | | Gross | length, | |
| 11361 | | | 19 | water line | 33ft |
| | | | | beam | 12.3ft |
| | | | | head room | 6.0ft |
| | | | | draught | 6.3ft |

| Construction | Place built | Date | Owner | Port of registration |
|---|---|---|---|---|
| Wood | Jersey | 1846 | Hilaire Belloc | Shoreham, Sussex |

But the boat had engraved (that is, cut into the wood) on her transom the words YACHT and, below that, JERSEY, signifying that the boat's name was 'Yacht' and her home port had been Jersey. The date of building was given as 1846. If that

Fig. 1.   The *Jersey*'s transom.

was correct, then Belloc had acquired an eighty-five-year-old boat as a gift from his friends.

He was proud of being able to say that she was the oldest yacht in Lloyd's Register. He did not keep up a yearly entry, however, probably because of the expense. I asked a staff member of Lloyd's whether it was a common practice to enter a yacht once only. She said 'Yes: we call them "vanity entries"'. Well, it was a pardonable piece of vanity on Hilaire Belloc's part, for as a boat for antiquarians the *Jersey* had much about her to be admired.

Through the kind advice of Mr Frank Carr, Chairman of the World Ship Trust, I have been able to trace some further facts about the past history of the *Jersey*, or 'Yacht' as she was actually called. The Assistant Harbour Master at St Helier, Jersey, unearthed an article in the Annual Bulletin of the Société Jersiaise, dated 1966, which brings us humanly closer to the old vessel. Captain F. B. Renouf, under the title 'AT THE TURN OF THE CENTURY, an old Jersey Sea Pilot Remembers', looks back some sixty years to when he first went to sea. A passage reads as follows:

> It was in January 1902 that I joined the Pilot Cutter 'Rival'. As apprentice I had to do the cooking for her five pilots – Thomas Roberts, the captain, Frank Renouf, George Renouf (my father), Phil Roberts and Mr Jack Allix. The other cutter, the 'Yacht', was manned by P. C. Renouf [see below], the captain, Edward

Larbalestier, Jack Larbalestier, George Roberts and Ernest Keeping. In those times each cutter was out on duty for three days, and brought ships in as they were sighted off the Corbière. In fine weather during the summer months we generally anchored in St Brelade's Bay, off Beauport, and when a ship appeared outside we got under weigh and put a pilot aboard. If we got rid of all our five pilots before the three days were up, we hoisted a large Pilot flag and sailed for home. This meant that the other cutter had to come on duty for three days – generally much to the crew's disgust, or ours, if the position was reversed.

We had a tough time in the winter months. We had to be on duty, no matter what the weather. When it was blowing hard from the west or south-west, we used to shelter under Belcroute in the lee of Noirmont beyond St Aubin's Fort. Then, when a ship appeared outside Noirmont Point, we would get under weigh, meet her and put the pilot on board out there, but, if the weather was too bad, she would have to sail on into the bay to get smoother water before this could be done. In the summer time, on the other hand, life in the cutter was ideal. Sometimes we would cruise all day with the mackerel lines out – down to St Ouen's Bay and as far as Grosnez. If it was our third day out, we all went home with a good feed of mackerel. And on a Sunday morning, anchored in St Brelade's Bay, we went around the lobster pots, and always had a good helping of lobsters and spider crabs. What would I not give now to have a feed of them!

I remember one winter night when we were anchored under Noirmont, I was sitting in the companionway, keeping a look out. Our time was up the next morning, and I knew that if the cutter had to get under weigh now we should carry on and go to our moorings in the old harbour. It happened that I had a mouth-organ with a low deep note on it that could sound like the whistle of a steamer coming around the Point. I blew. Then I listened for movement down below. I blew again. Then I heard Jack Allix sing out to my uncle, 'Do you hear that, Frank?' I blew again and they all fell for it. We got under weigh in a strong wind, opened the Point and could see the Corbière light flashing. No sign of any steamer. My uncle said, 'We might as well run off home'. So I gained an extra night home – at 'Pilot View' beyond Commercial Buildings – which suited me as I was courting at the time.

This gives us a picture of Belloc's *Jersey* (née 'Yacht') at the turn of the century, working as a pilot and then aged fifty-six years.

The island of Jersey had a thriving maritime life in the nineteenth century and a great number of ships were built there. John Jean, in his plentifully illustrated and well-documented account of this activity, *Jersey Sailing Ships*, gives a list of about 1,600 Jersey Sea Captains, with the names of their ships, sometimes their spouses and the year of their captaincy.[1] They are nearly all old French names. There are twenty-five Renoufs! F. B. Renouf, the author of this 1966 article, is listed as Master of the training ship *Botha*, South Africa, 1921. And P. C. Renouf, Captain of the 'Yacht' given in the excerpt, appears in a list of fifty-two names of Jersey pilots of the nineteenth century. Quite a large number of pilots were employed; in 1852, for example, there were twenty-eight serving on the west and eight on the east coasts of the island. Pilot boats are not named in John Jean's book, which deals with two-masted and three-masted vessels, except two of 30 tons each in 1830, one of them skippered by yet another Renouf. It is good to know that Belloc's *Jersey* played a part in all this vanished world of sail and trade in the Channel Islands.

Mr J. H. Arrowsmith, Assistant Registrar of British Ships, St Helier, has kindly given me the following chronicle of the 'Yacht' from the records of Jersey's registry:

1846: Built at St Martin during this year.

1847: Registered by John Richardson, Mariner, as Master and sole owner. Dimensions on survey were length 34.9 feet, breadth 11.1 feet, depth 6.1 feet, tonnage 14, a cutter with running bowsprit and square stern. (Compare these measurements with the later survey and those of Lloyd's Register – the discrepancy may be due to the adding of a counter to the square stern, perhaps in two stages?)

1854: Sold to Philip Mollet Jnr, Mariner.

1862: Sold by Mollet to Philip Renouf Jnr, John Sampson, Charles

---

[1] John Jean, *Jersey Sailing Ships* (Phillimore: Chichester, 1982).

Larbalestier and William Keeping, Pilots, each with sixteen shares. (The name Larbalestier is derived from *arbalestier*, an old French word for a crossbowman, and would originally have been spelt l'Arbalestier.)

1874:   Sampson's shares sold to P. C. Renouf.

1878:   Surveyed. Length 36.5 feet, breadth 12.3 feet, depth 6.05 feet, tons 12.98.

1907:   Ownership divided between ten pilots and in the ensuing years several pilots owned her.

The records of the Registry of British Ships continue:

1928:   The 'Yacht' was acquired by Frank Lawrence, Fisherman, as sole owner, who sold her on the same day, 13 July, to John White Reynolds.

1930:   Sold by J. W. Reynolds on 14 January to Osny Lonsdale Parsons, of Hayling Island.

1932:   Sold by Parsons to Hilaire Belloc on 28 April.

In fact, according to letters he wrote at the time, it was in April 1931 that Mr Belloc had the boat refitted in Chichester Harbour, and he went sailing in her that summer. But it is possible that the final registration of the sale and new ownership was not made until 1932. It is rather remarkable that the records of so small a craft, relative to the schooners and two- or three-masted ships built in Jersey in the nineteenth century, should have been kept in such detail.

When Belloc became the last captain of the old cutter, he referred to her in his letters as 'the famous hulk'. She did, alas, become a hulk eventually, but not until he had given her another lease of life and she had reached the age of a hundred years, in 1946 – so splendidly had this old wooden ship been built a century before.

The end of the record is as follows:

1947:   In the first post-war edition of Lloyd's Register of Yachts the vessel appears as JERSEY, owned by G. E. Mackenzie, who had bought her from Hilaire Belloc in a hulk-like condition in 1946 (see page 157).

1954:   The vessel appears as YACHT, same owner.

1955:   The *Jersey* disappears from Lloyd's Register from this year onwards.

### A DESCRIPTION OF THE *JERSEY*

It is or was characteristic of the Channel Islands to strike a note in domestic architecture, and probably in boat construction also, half-way between the English and the French styles. French fishing boats have traditionally had a steeply raking transom and sternpost, a sheer rising to high bluff bows and a keel running straight from forefoot to sternpost, falling steeply to give the maximum depth at a point about two-thirds of the length

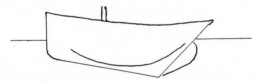

Typical profile of a French fishing boat

Plank-on-edge type of English nineteenth-century yacht

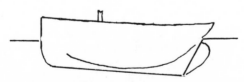

Approximate profile of the *Jersey*

Fig. 2. Some traditional profiles.

of the boat from the bows. They are very heavily built with massive frames throughout. They have not only to stand the strains of pounding in heavy seas but jostle with other boats in crowded fishing ports and grind their keels on the floors of harbours that dry out and often lie high and dry taking their full weight on their bilges.

The *Jersey* on the other hand was built for more speed, to be more handy under sail, to stay at sea in all kinds of weather, hove-to or making sail, to put her pilots aboard incoming ships and get back to port (St Helier) with only two men or probably a man and boy. She would also have berthed apart, permanently afloat, not taking the ground like a fishing boat. Therefore she did not have quite such heavy construction; nevertheless her oak frames, which were visible in the unpanelled forward part of the ship, were splendid and though some wet rot could be seen in a few places you felt that she would never break up whatever conditions the sea might inflict on her, or whatever might give way through age and time in her rigging or deck structures.

Her sternpost and transom were not so steeply raked and the drop of her long straight keel from stern to sternpost was not so deep. Underwater she was full bodied, rather bold in the shoulders with a fine belly amidships, tapering smoothly to the sternpost, very little of her transom being below the water line. Her flush deck was of teak planks about 2½ inches wide, laid straight fore and aft with no 'onion-skin' curvature paralleling the shape of the hull, as in gentlemen's yachts of the old days, which is the pride of all top-class boats whether of wood or fibreglass today. The only structures that interrupted this wide expanse of teak were the windlass and capstan, a square hatch on the foredeck, the mast, the companion and a rectangular coach roof about 4 feet by 3 feet, giving light to the after cabin.

The stern of the *Jersey* ended with a slight 'tumble-home' of the topsides, blended into a short counter, through which the stout rudder post appeared. The 'hole' through which the rudder post passed up through the deck – the rudder trunk – was kidney-shaped in section to allow full rotation of the post with the pull of the tiller. It was lined by vertical strips of teak, a very fine piece of construction. The wooden bulwarks were 14 inches high in the bows, tapering to 11 inches at the counter.

What gave the *Jersey* her ancient look were the shrouds, rat-lines, dead-eyes and chain-plates. Three steel wire stays, the shrouds, gave lateral support to the mast each side. They were parcelled and served with tarred hemp from end to end and covered with bitumen, which gave a smooth surface to grip hold of when climbing up the rigging by means of the rat-lines which were strung between them. This rope-ladder is the traditional

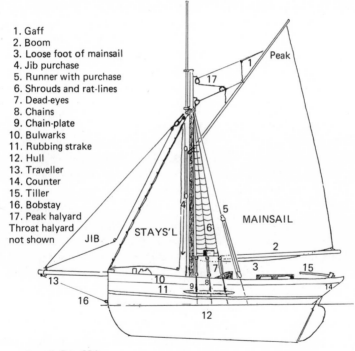

1. Gaff
2. Boom
3. Loose foot of mainsail
4. Jib purchase
5. Runner with purchase
6. Shrouds and rat-lines
7. Dead-eyes
8. Chains
9. Chain-plate
10. Bulwarks
11. Rubbing strake
12. Hull
13. Traveller
14. Counter
15. Tiller
16. Bobstay
17. Peak halyard
Throat halyard
not shown

Length OA: 38 ft
Length WL: 33 ft
Beam: 12.3 ft
Draught: 6.3 ft

Fig. 3. The yacht *Jersey*.

means by which sailors went aloft to handle sails. We used the rat-lines a great deal. It was very useful to be able to go up to the masthead to clear or repair something, to grab a loose halyard, for a lookout or for pleasure. It was a safer business at sea to climb up the shrouds than going up in a bos'n's chair which is the only way possible now, in yachts.

The spread of the shrouds, and therefore the staying power, was increased by wooden projections, the chain-plates, from the ship's side. Three steel strops bolted to the ship's timbers held the pull of the shrouds and were linked by iron rods about 2 feet long which passed up through the chain-plate to the dead-eyes (see fig. 3). These were round blocks of wood bored with three holes, through which tarred hemp passed six times like a tackle and was pulled to the requisite tautness. This gave great strength and slight elasticity when the shrouds took the strain. There were also runners a very short way aft of the shrouds. This was the way all old-time sailing vessels were rigged.

The *Jersey*'s navigation lights were splendid things. The base containing the paraffin can and burner was about 8 inches square. The green or the red glass globe through which the light shone filled an 8-inch square frame. The height of the whole lamp from base to dome and chimney was about 16 inches. The boards on which they were slung were fixed to the shrouds 5 feet above the deck. The shrouds on the lee side were rather loose when we were sailing on the wind and the lamp jerked and oscillated a bit, but it never went out. We carried these lights in some night passages in quite strong winds and they never blew out. It was always a proud moment when, having lit them in the cabin and allowed them to warm up, they were brought on deck at the fall of night and hoisted into their positions. There is nothing more beautiful at sea at night than a sailing vessel, whose sails can dimly be made out, with its red navigation light or the glow-worm green of a starboard light and no other lamps showing, silently moving by. Compared to this the lights of powered ships with whirring dynamos, beautiful though they are, seem garish and fussy.

Fig. 4. The *Jersey*'s binnacle was a square frame with a pyramidal cover,
the side facing the helmsman being made of glass. The little colza lamp
shed a light from the right side onto the compass card.

The binnacle was a brass box fixed on the top of the coach
roof of the after cabin with a pyramidal lid covering the compass in its gimbals. The after face of the pyramid was of glass.
The compass card was illuminated at night by a little lamp on one
side. This, I was told by an aged salt in some port, was a colza
burner. When Hilaire Belloc wrote (concerning the whale):

> But you may cut its blubber up
> And melt it down for oil
> And so replace the colza bean
> A product of the soil

he cannot have known that colza oil was considered to give the
perfect light for binnacle lamps or he would surely have mentioned it. And its replacement by whale oil could hardly be
considered a mark of progress. When I first became acquainted
with the lamp, I tried to get colza oil at a ship's chandler but they
had had none for years. The lamp worked beautifully with
paraffin and never blew out.

The main hatchway or companion was amidships. Below
decks what struck you on descending the steps were the six
berths for pilots, three each side from amidships to the stern.
They were painted white. The stern bunks were small, more

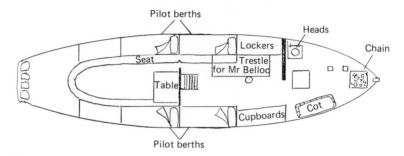

Fig. 5. The *Jersey*'s layout below decks; roomy but with few amenities.
There was no chart table and no galley.

suitable for boys. We used them chiefly for personal gear. But
the others were quite roomy and Mr Belloc had had good
thick horse hair mattresses fitted in each. They were really
comfortable. He was not agile enough to climb into any of them
himself and had therefore had a special bed made which unfolded
from the port side like a table, with legs to support it; about 6½
feet long and 3½ feet wide. He lay on a large inflatable rubber
mattress. The after part of the ship was separated off by a
windowed partition to which a small flap of table was hinged.
Under it a stone demijohn of water was kept and on it some

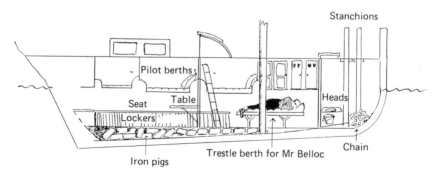

Fig. 6. The *Jersey*'s accommodation below decks.

· 36 ·

primus cooking was done. The primus stove was often put on the cabin floor for safety as there were no gimbals belonging to it. All the woodwork in the after cabin was painted white except the seat below the bunks, with lockers under, which was of some dark polished wood and ran round the cabin in a U-shape, keeping the curve of the stern. The main cabin, if you could call it such, was the sitting or standing space into which you descended by the main hatch. It was about 8 feet wide and looking forwards was open right up to the bows, except for a partition on the port side behind which was what I can only call a 'sea-privy', known in the Navy as 'the heads'.

The mast, bristling with rotary pumps attached to it, seemed to occupy a lot of living space. There was no central cabin table; a pity, for the after-cabin table was a mere shelf to put things on and you could not sit round it. As it was we sat on the side benches in the main and after cabins and often put mugs or plates on the floor. Access to the fo'c's'le to the right of the mast was easy and with the forehatch open ventilation was good. The ship's timbers were uncovered forward of the mast and a splendid sight they were.

Below the floorboards in her enormous bilge there was a vast amount of internal ballast in the form of huge iron pigs, coated with slimy orange rust. The bilge water when you pumped her out was always like soup; brown Windsor to begin with, turning to thick tomato as you got down to the dregs.

The *Jersey* always leaked. Even when the worst flaws in her planking were repaired she continued to leak a good deal. Her own original pump may well have dated from her construction in 1846. It was a pipe of about 2 inches in calibre from bilge to deck, running up beside the mast and expanding into a cylinder of 3 inches in diameter which had its open end on deck beside the mast. The plunger with its leather flap valve was fitted with a long iron T-shaped puller. You primed the plunger with half a bucketful of water and then, standing astride the hole, holding the T-piece with two hands and using arm, back and leg muscles, sucked frantically till the 'soup' came up from the depths and flowed over the deck and away under the scuppers. Once you got into a good rhythm and your muscles attuned, it would throw up about a pint a stroke and at the start, at any rate, you could do sixty strokes a minute. We called it the 'gut-stretcher'. It was very tiring but two men could share the work, each with a hand on the puller. There was also a rotary pump in the cabin for more leisurely pumping, which was little effort but very slow. Later on, when the leaking was bad and an aged caretaker complained of the strain of the gut-stretcher, a very big rotary pump was installed, also fixed on the mast, so the *Jersey* ended up with three pumps. And as it turned out there were a few critical occasions when all three were needed together.

The *Jersey*'s sails had belonged to a Brixham trawler. They fitted almost perfectly, except for the tops'l. Brixham trawlers have a forward-raking mast which has the effect of making a gaff mainsail a more pressing, harder-driving sail when dragging a trawl. The outer end of the boom is thereby lifted, the foot of the sail rises from tack to clew. But the *Jersey*'s mast was vertical and therefore the foot of the mainsail was horizontal, likewise the boom, rather than tucked up as in the trawler. Mr Belloc disliked a low boom, difficult for him to dodge in a tack or a gybe, so he had the *Jersey*'s raised some 5 feet above the deck at the mast. I always disliked the appearance this gave her; I don't know why, a high horizontal boom, or worse still a boom whose outer end sags below the horizontal, is unsightly to me. The outer end of a boom which may swing fast or violently should be well clear of the heads of the crew. A well tucked-up boom is correct and looks business-like and lively. Boats have 'sex appeal' according to their shape and rig. A sagging boom is dowdy. When I sailed the *Jersey* with my friends, I brought the forward end of the boom down, pulled the tack down lower and set the peak up high to give a set more like the trawler. It looked good and I'll swear she liked it.

Below the water line the *Jersey* was copper-sheathed down to her keel. It had been beautifully done at some distant date in the past, perhaps when she was built. When the leak problem seemed insoluble in the late 1930s it was a moot point whether or not to have the copper off to inspect her seams properly and recaulk them. In the end we left it.

The running rigging was standard for a boat of this size with heavy tanned Brixham trawler sails, that is to say the jib and peak halyards each had a free end and a fixed end with a purchase on it. The purchase was a two-block tackle with two sheaves each and four strands of thinner rope. You hoisted the jib to a reasonable tautness and finished the job by hauling down on the purchase. There were no mast winches, but the purchase was a powerful tackle and did the job. When lowering sails, you had to remember to let up the purchase first so as to have a good down haul in hand the next time the sail was set. Otherwise you might find the upper block coming right down to the lower, and the jib still not taut; a condition known as 'chock-a-block'. Mr Belloc liked this expression. He also liked the expression 'ramshackle', which was apt for some of the *Jersey*'s shackles and her general state as a seagoing vessel.

The throat halyard of the mainsail worked through two splendid lignum vitae, double-sheave blocks. No purchase was necessary because after the jaws of the gaff were hoisted to the required height the luff of the mainsail was made very taut by a powerful tack purchase. These wooden blocks had a ratchet in them that made a throaty rattling sound as the sail was hoisted up. It was the cheerful sound of getting under way and in those days could be heard in fishing harbours at any time of day or night, but for me it always recalls yachts, summer, the setting of sails and the thrill of departure. There are different sounds now which are also becoming nostalgic, the click of mast winches and the fishing-reel ring of deck winches, but nothing quite so exciting as the rattle of old wooden blocks and tackles.

The *Jersey*'s bowsprit was a 20-foot spar: 7 feet of it was inboard and square-ended, 13 feet of it projected outboard, a menace to all shipping. It was held between stout bitts and its inward thrust was checked by a huge wooden pin or spiggot which traversed its full square thickness. The jib was hauled out to the tip of the bowsprit on a 'traveller', a leather-covered iron ring about 9 inches in diameter bearing a hook with a twist in it. This held the eye of the foot of the jib and never let it come off.

The *Jersey* had a pair of 'legs' for use in drying-out harbours. These were stout balks of timber 8 feet long and 6 inches square in section. They were capped by a metal fitting with a tongue which projected upwards and fitted into a slot in the chain-plates. The leg was maintained in the vertical position by guy ropes from the foot to the bow and stern. Both legs could be fitted on one side of the boat when alongside a quay, giving extra security at low tide. The legs were used only a few times, notably in Folkestone Harbour. They took up deck space and were in the end discarded.

### THE WINDLASS

It may have been cumbersome but its power was immense. The strong wooden posts that held the great drum and cogwheels were bolted to the timbers down in the fo'c's'le and to the deck beams, above which they rose about 3 feet. Two bitts (a,a$^1$) formed the housing of the bowsprit, giving it lateral stability and providing stanchions for the belaying of warps when mooring in harbour or riding to a kedge or being towed. Two wooden side-pieces (b,b$^1$) contained between them the barrel of the

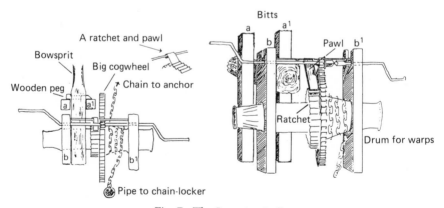

Fig. 7. The *Jersey*'s windlass

windlass and, projecting on their outer sides, on the same axle were wooden drums for the winching in of warps or for any heavy pulling with ropes. The power was derived from a cog-wheel of 2 feet in diameter on the axle of the drum, which was driven by one very small cogwheel turned by using iron handles which fitted into it from either side of the windlass. When two men exerted the strength of their backs together, the pull that this winch could exert, if the chain did not slip, was very powerful. The recoil of the drum under strain was checked by a ratchet and pawl. The pawl made a merry chink-clink-clink as you wound. And that is another of the magical sounds of getting under way which is hardly ever heard today.

By the way, the chain passed up from the chain-locker, three times round the drum and forward to the anchor. There was no means of casting it off the drum except by unshackling it from the anchor and hauling it back over the drum three times. All yachts have to lay out chain on deck before coming to anchor, to let go for the initial drop. In the *Jersey* you had to pull it over the windlass three times to have enough ready to run out. Once the anchor was down and the chain taking the strain, you could lift the pawl off the ratchet and let the drum unwind, easing the chain up from below and over the drum by hand. Mr Belloc was exasperated by all this and had a large capstan installed between the windlass and the mast. Turns of chain could be thrown on or cast off it in a moment. It was not so powerful but very much more practical. Unfortunately it went overboard, in odd cir-cumstances told in these pages, and we had to put up with the windlass for the rest of the old boat's life.

# MR BELLOC AT POOLE
# ABOARD THE *JERSEY*

ON the appointed day in July 1931 I took a train to Poole. The weather was what is called unsettled and typical of this monsoon month of the English climate, when the holiday season begins. I travelled alone. Mr Belloc and others were already there, preparing for the sail to westward. The town of Poole is bounded on the north and west sides by water. It had pleasant old streets and tall warehouses in its north-west corner, round the docks, and tailed away as an uninteresting township towards the south-east. It was in those days a busy port for small traders. There is a very long quay on the west side against which small ships loaded and unloaded. As I passed along it in my search for the *Jersey*, to my delight I came upon a Brittany onion boat. She was a yawl 50 feet or more in length with an immense gaff mainsail. Ropes of onions slung on poles were ranged along the deck, glowing in the sun. Here and there about the ship were several young boys with berets, who would soon be bicycling inland with the onions on poles over their shoulders, even travelling up to London. My father was never able to resist their French charm when they appeared in Chelsea and he would often come home to dinner in the late summer carrying one of these beautiful swags of golden onions only to be ridiculed by our cook for the price he had paid for it.

I found the *Jersey* afloat off the yard of a shipwright called Shutler and boarded by a gangplank. My first impression of her, with her black paint, heavy shrouds, tanned sails, very heavy tackle and enormous deck space was of a smack, but one soon came to see that she had certain refinements of line and never had been a fishing boat. The weight of my stepping aboard caused only the slightest swing of the mast against the sky. This was impressive to a sailor of small boats like me. A great green tarpaulin had been stretched over the boom to make a tent and there inside, sitting on a box, was Mr Belloc. He explained as he welcomed me in that the decks were leaking so abominably that it was the only way of keeping the cabin dry and 'the ruffian, Shutler' had done nothing about it. It was too late to caulk them now and we would have to go to sea with drips in our bunks. He was in black as usual, but in a very thick cloth.

The wind was cold, it was showery weather and he kept his cloak on, but was bare-headed, showing his grizzled, freshly crew-cut hair. I immediately joined in with the business in hand, the stowing of provisions, and in so doing met the three members of the crew who had arrived before me. They were A. D. Peters, the literary agent and head of the firm (which still continues under his name after his death in 1973), harvester of royalties of Hilaire Belloc's literary works and hawk for his interests; and Bill Aitkin, introduced to Mr Belloc by A. D. Peters and invited to come on the cruise to make up the manpower, though with no great experience of the sea. A. D. Peters knew even less about sailing for that matter, and made fun of himself about it most of the time when hauling or fastening ropes. And there was Peter Belloc, the youngest of Mr Belloc's five children, who had experience of sailing going back to the *Nona* days. Peter had the hereditary Bellocian high spirits, which had now broken forth with his sudden liberation on holiday from Fleet Street, and was helping to cheer his father up, who seemed depressed by the rain and the tarpaulin.

The provisions were strewn all over the place under the shelter of the tarpaulin and were gradually being passed down below to be stowed. There was a great deal of stuff but of very limited variety, viz. large tins of julienne soup, corned beef, butter in tins and a pickle called 'Savora', a fiery yellow mixture of onions and raw cauliflower. There was a great pile of bread, two dozen or so of large tin loaves, enough to feed ten men for a week or longer. Having once run out of bread at sea, Mr Belloc had sworn he would never again make the mistake of not having ample stocks of this, the cheapest and easiest obtainable food. At the end of another cruise I was to see a similar overprovision of loaves jettisoned, floating away, hard as bricks, mildewed and inedible.

Mr Belloc did not believe that it was possible to cook at sea in a sailing boat nor worth the trouble to make a dish of any sort, especially of meat, although he was very French, liked good food and knew about cooking. Indeed there had been a time when, if invited to dinner, he liked to propose to come and cook it or prepare a special dish. My mother once endured this experience. There was such turmoil and noise down in the basement that she did not know what was going on, and when the dinner was over and the guests had left, she went down and found the kitchen in utter confusion, things on the floor, every utensil used and left unwashed, sauces spilt, chaos. Her sister, Charlotte Balfour, had had the same experience once and never allowed it again.

No wonder, then, that he thought cooking could not be carried on in boats. We lived off corned beef, pickles and julienne soup heated on a primus stove, ignoring the dozens of delicious thick soups and stews that were to be had in tins. Ah, but there was the wine, dozens of good dark bottles, without labels, bottled at King's Land on the ground floor of the mill from an imported cask. Splendid full-bodied stuff it turned out to be. Water was in two very fine oak kegs on deck holding about four gallons each and a stone demijohn in the cabin. But we had little use for it except for coffee, certainly not for washing.

It was not until my third sail in the *Jersey* that anyone complained of there not being any means of having a good wash. This was George Bowles, Commander RN (retired), who came with us on the cross-Channel cruise described in 'Boulogne,

Crossing the Colbart, Crécy, Fog'. He was a charming, kindly man whose courteous manners were a model for embassies or palaces but which seemed none the less absolutely natural to life aboard a ramshackle old boat because of the laughter with which he accompanied everything he did or said, and because Hilaire Belloc himself was an extremely courteous man. George Bowles was one of those people who are easily amused. After everything he said or heard, he burst out laughing. This suggests a state of perpetual fatuity. Not at all, he was a man of subtle humour and wit, but there were these guffaws every time he made a remark, whether or not it was funny. He liked to wash now and again, and though he was too polite to complain to Mr Belloc that there was no means of doing so, he did complain, with many bursts of laughter, to us. He was writing a book at the time on the Roman bath and astonished us with his account of the grandeur and colossal dimensions of the baths of ancient Rome which had existed or had been planned but were too big to be built. He lectured us on the virtue of the bath by steam followed by cleansing in running water and on the squalor of the modern household bath in which you lay in a sort of soup of your own dirt and then dabbed it off with a towel. The title of his book was to be *No Bath Yet* (guffaw).

When we got to Boulogne on that cruise and went ashore for provisions, he purchased and brought aboard a huge enamel basin which he dumped on the cabin table. I do not think Mr Belloc was put out, he seemed hardly to notice it. And I do not think anyone, except George Bowles, used it for washing – there was not enough water. On acquiring the boat Mr Belloc had said that 'it will be good to have some frills which make the boat habitable', but I am afraid George Bowles' enamel basin was the nearest thing the *Jersey* ever got to one. Hilaire Belloc was fundamentally a gipsy when at sea, as is suggested by his remark in *The Cruise of the Nona*: 'the pleasant little cabin of the *Nona* (pleasant to me, odious to the pernickety, for it is a hugger-mugger home) . . .'

Other sanitary arrangements were also primitive. Nature's

needs were met by the sea, when at sea, or by a half partition in the forward part of the cabin, near the fo'c's'le hatch, hiding a seat with a hole in it and a bucket with a rope attached to its handle. You drew a bucketful of sea water from over the side, lowered it into the fo'c's'le through the hatch and went below and took it behind the partition. Later you hauled the bucket up again through the forehatch and – slosh, over the side; the leeward side. In spite of the extraordinary efficiency of the pumping lavatories of modern yachts, which have taken years of research to perfect, I often hanker after the good old bucket which was so simple and healthy.

I did not think the sleeping arrangements Mr Belloc had made for himself were nearly as comfortable as the pilots' berths occupied by us. There was no boarding to keep him in if the ship rolled and he never looked fully at ease to me. He lay down with a black silk scarf bandaging his eyes, looking rather like a prisoner on the scaffold before the execution, but supine. If he wanted to read in the night, which was often, because he slept badly, he lit a little double candlestick that he always took with him on his travels. It was silver-plated and resembled a miniature ship's ventilator cowl. Two candle flames burnt within the hollow of the cowl and the shining silver of the inner surface reflected the light down on to his book. A pair of chimneys in the roof of the

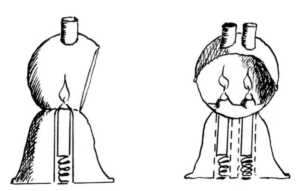

Fig. 8. Mr Belloc's two-candle-power reflector lamp.

cowl, one over each flame, allowed smoke and excess heat to escape upwards.

By way of a dinghy, so that we could get ourselves ashore from a mooring, Mr Shutler had provided an enormous rowing boat at least 15 feet long and much too big to take on deck. This would have to be towed wherever we went. Little did we know, however, as we settled into our berths that first night aboard, what this brute of a jolly-boat would have in store for us.

# THE ANVIL POINT AFFAIR

I F they are to understand the Anvil Point affair, a preliminary
digression is necessary for those unfamiliar with the sailing of
boats. It concerns 'gybing'.

The word 'gybe' comes from an old Dutch verb *gijben*. The
word spelt 'jibe' or 'gibe' (Shorter Oxford Dictionary) comes,
apparently, from an old French word meaning 'to handle roughly
in sport', to jeer, utter taunts or flout. HB was fond of a gibe
against doctors, for example:

> They murmured as they took their fees
> There is no cure for this disease.

It looks as if the literary or colloquial use of gibe was derived from
the nautical term (as so many are) for metaphorically they are
much the same. He who is the object of the gibe feels roughly
handled or taunted, as the mariner does whose mainsail suddenly
goes across the deck with a bang.

But what is 'to gybe' at sea? When a boat is sailing with the
wind coming from behind, the mainsail is let out, with the boom
at right-angles to the body of the boat, or nearly so. It thus
presents its maximum area to the wind. The mainsail is, of
course, equally effective on either side when the wind is in the mid
line, aft. The manœuvre of gybing is to change the mainsail over

Hilaire Belloc in 1933, aged 63, photographed by Jim Hall.

Mr Belloc with the ironical gleam in his eye.

'Shall we turn to the breezier Belloc?' (Stevie Smith)

It was always easy to go up the masthead using the
shrouds and rat-lines

The *Jersey* in Shoreham Harbour.

The *Jersey* leaving the Solent in the summer of 1933.

Setting the tops'l, which did not fit, as the topmast was short. The shape of the hull is well seen.

A.D. Peters working the captstan.

The Old Man 'out on the salt' again. Note the leather boots, watch chain and pince-nez.

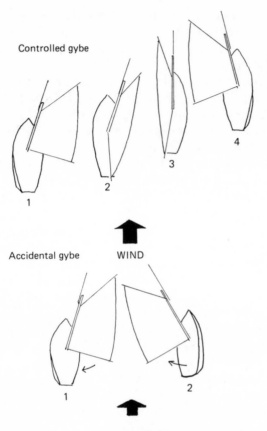

Fig. 9. Gybing.

from one side to the other, because a change in the direction of the wind or an alteration of the boat's course demands it. The boom is brought in to the mid line by hauling on the sheet, and securely held there. When the wind catches the sail on the other side (aback) it blows it across suddenly. But the boom is tightly held and the sheet is let out gradually, so no harm is done.

A sudden, unprepared gybe, however; an accidental, mistaken, careless gybe, caused by a dreaming helmsman or a freak gust of wind from the wrong direction or a wave giving a twist to the boat's course through the water, may do great damage. The mainsail flies from one side to the other, swinging the boom violently across the deck. Anyone standing up and looking the wrong way and slow to react to the shout of 'Gybe O!', 'Watch out' or 'Duck' may be stunned by a blow on the side of the head or knocked overboard. In its unbridled violence the boom may smash the lee runner and the mast is in peril. Masts have indeed gone overboard when a gybe has occurred by accident in a sudden squall.

Anyone in a modern Bermuda-rigged yacht that gybes, even accidentally, may wonder what all the fuss is about. The Bermuda mainsail is comparatively harmless; not so the gaff sail. The old-time mainsails with their long gaffs and long booms could have a tremendous weight of wind in them. Besides, ships and small craft of the great days of sail were often old, too old still to be sailing; fastenings broke, their rigging tore, their sails split; they had to gybe with care. The *Jersey* belonged to those great days. She too was old, perhaps too old; we did not know what shocks she could take. Mr Belloc had sailed only in old boats. The *Nona* was a fine old one, but ramshackle. I have no doubt he gybed with care and, you may be sure, accidentally too. Anyhow, he was nervous about gybing.

The morning after our arrival at Poole we set sail for a passage westward, to Weymouth, but we were never to reach that port owing to an incident at Anvil Point near St Albans Head off the Dorset coast. That evening, in fact, a rueful Mr Belloc and his crew would be back in Poole Harbour. It was an exciting incident in which disaster to the ship, danger to Mr Belloc and ourselves, even drowning, stared us in the face for a few minutes.

The first leg of the passage from Poole to Weymouth is due south to Durlston Head, about six sea miles. You pass two splendid sandy bays, Studland and Swanage, separated by a promontory on the east-facing coast of the Isle of Purbeck. Off this promontory stands one of those tall pillars of rock which are to be found all round our coasts, which the sea seems unable to bring down though the cliffs behind it have long ago crumbled and retreated, leaving the rock to fight it out alone. 'Old Harry, my children,' Mr Belloc said, as the pillar came into view on leaving the mouth of Poole Harbour, and we steered a course just to the east of it.

The wind was due west and moderate, but with signs of freshening. The sky was cloudy. It had been a fair wind for leaving, taking us round Brownsea Island at great speed with full sail set. The *Jersey* heeled but not uncomfortably. With her great beam she thought nothing of it. She was stiff. Mr Shutler's huge dinghy foamed along behind with painter taut and nose in air. It must have been a lovely sight.

There is about a mile of moorings along the curve of the eastern shore of Poole Harbour on which lie hundreds of boats of all kinds. In the 1930s there were some graceful yachts among them, but also the most hideous motor boats and nondescript craft which the rapidly expanding yachting industry had produced for any man with a bit of money to get to sea in or live aboard in harbour. And here flying past them, with eighty-five years of history between us and them, with her tanned sails, and black hull and rigging, was this fine old cutter, such as you may find depicted in many of Turner's seascapes. People on the beach or looking out of motor-boat cabins would also have noticed on the deck of this apparition a stocky figure clad all in black with grizzled head, seeming also to belong to the past.

On the ebb tide the huge ramifying estuary of Poole pours its waters out through the narrow exit at Sandbanks, not at the furious and dangerous speed of the Morbihan in Brittany, a similar estuary with a bigger tidal rise and fall, but still – quite a dizzy glide. So out we went, in high spirits, pointing for Old Harry, the *Jersey* like an old Shire horse feeling the harness again and pulling with all her weight. Wine was brought up and poured into enamel mugs, pint mugs. No, they were not filled to the brim, you just kept an eye on what was left in the bottle.

It took a bit over an hour to get to Durlston Head, then Mr Belloc spoke in this manner:

Now my children, we are getting near St Albans Head and the tide race off the headland, which extends a good mile out to sea. It's not as bad as Portland race, nothing like so rough, so surprising or dangerous and horrible as Portland race, but still we'll try and avoid the worst of it by keeping close to the land. It's not so rough off the head as it is farther out. It's the right thing to do, especially with the wind against the tide.

Durlston Head is the corner of a square area of country, the Isle of Purbeck, and the coast runs westward from here to Weymouth Bay in a straight line for twenty miles, except for the promontory of St Albans, about five miles on, sticking about a mile out to sea; a considerable cape for small sailing craft in a headwind, even with a fair tide. Little did we know, however, that we should not get round it that day and that a much smaller promontory just to the east of it, the Anvil, was going to bar the way.

Once round Durlston Head our course was west; so was the wind and it was freshening. The seas were steep, the *Jersey* tossed and plunged and seemed to like it but went much slower as we hauled in the sheets and pointed her up into the wind, sailing south-west.

Soon we were getting too far out for Mr Belloc's plan of keeping along the coast, so we tacked and headed north-west towards the high cliffs of Purbeck. The *Jersey* came about all right that time, helped round by backing the jib. She was standing up stiffly to the freshening breeze. The steeper seas were rebuffed by her heavy bows with a thud and a swishing sound. She kept going well, though not very fast, three knots perhaps.

'Now my children,' Mr Belloc cried when we were getting rather close to the cliffs, 'we must go about and try to clear St Albans on the other tack.' He sat on the coach roof amidships, an excellent position for the skipper at all times. Peter Belloc was setting. Bill Aitken, A. D. Peters and I were ready with the jib and stays'l sheets and runners (Runners, by the way, are additional stays to the mast which have to be set up taut on the windward side and slackened on the leeward side. They were a nuisance to attend to, but the mast of an old ship like the *Jersey* needed their support at all times.)

Peter put the helm over and shouted 'Lee O!' The jib sheets were let loose and rather slowly she came up into the wind. The old war-horse dipped and tossed and rattled her harness. Then she plunged into a trough and heaved at the next wave; she was slowing down. We were dead in the eye of the wind. She stopped. Then she fell back on the original course. We had missed stays, we had failed to come about. 'What's wrong?' Mr Belloc shouted. 'Why did she miss? Not enough way on. You must drive her harder, Peter. It must be the drag of that infernal dinghy.'

So we headed once more for the rocky cliffs, now only about

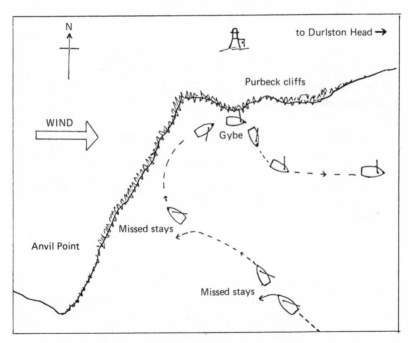

Fig. 10. Anvil Point and the Purbeck cliffs.

200 yards away. Anvil Point was right ahead, dark against the westward sky. On the chart it had seemed nothing, but now it barred the way ahead and we were driving straight into the angle made by this promontory and the cliffs of the Purbeck shore, into a corner from which there was no escape except by successfully getting on to the other tack or by bearing right away until the wind was aft, gybing, if indeed there was room to do so, and running before the wind parallel to the rocks, then steering out to sea again with the mainsail on the landward side; in brief, by gybing round and away.

The second attempt to come about also failed. The *Jersey* was really carrying too much sail, for the wind was now freshening all the time, but in spite of getting good speed on before turning up into the wind she slowed, plunged and stopped as before. She would not come round and began once again to go backwards. 'Reverse your helm, *r*everse your helm!' Mr Belloc shouted to Peter. But it was no good. She was blown back on her original course, pointing at the cliffs again. It was a crisis. The cliffs were very close. A break in the clouds at this moment let through the sun which made the cliffs ahead blacker, the seas greener, the foam whiter and our alarmed faces clearer. To attempt yet again to go about appeared to me to be doomed to failure and far too risky. There was nothing for it but to gybe immediately; but was there room to turn?

'We must gybe, Sir!' I shouted to Mr Belloc.

'Oh my dear, do you think so? Do you think she'll stand it? It's too dange*r*ous, she won't stand it!'

'Well, can I try?' I said.

'Yes, yes, go on then or we're lost.'

I took the tiller from Peter, pulled it hard up (to port) and shouted to the others to let the mainsheet run right out so that the mainsail would have less power. Even so it began to drive her at a furious speed towards the cliffs on our lee side. As the speed increased the rudder became more effective. I pulled the helm aweather for dear life, for all our lives! She began to turn away from the wind, but still not away from the rocks. Would there be room? Why wouldn't she turn in a tighter circle, the brute? God, what weather helm she had! I pulled and I pulled. I thought she could just reach the gybing point before crashing on to the rocks, now about thirty yards away.

At critical moments like this one is intensely aware of many things besides the danger and the action necessary to save oneself. A great noise came from those cliffs. It was the rumble of big surf running high up on to the rocks, the splashing of the water cascading back into the sea, the hiss of foam and the echoing clamour of seagulls. These sounds, wonderful sounds, are familiar to anyone who has clambered on cliffs or down into rocky bays, but from the deck of a yacht they came as a shock. 'The shores are sounding things', Hilaire Belloc wrote in *The Silence of the Sea*. By God they are! The air too was full of spray and the smell of seaweed. At last the wind was dead astern and we could make the gybe and escape. Now for it! I shouted to Peters and Aitken to haul in on the mainsheet as quickly as possible to get that boom under control amidships before it slammed over. 'Take a turn of the rope round the big cleat,' I shouted. 'Check it from running out when the slam-over comes, and then let it out gradually. Don't let it go with a rip.' Alas, the grand slam came suddenly and too soon. A sea made the ship lurch and over went the mainsail with a bang. The mainsheet snatched the cleat right out of the deck, ripped through the hands of both crewmen, though they were gripping it tightly, and the boom crashed against the lee runner, which parted.

Peter immediately set up the weather runner and the mast was secured. The gybe was done, the crisis past; we were safe, and now with a following wind, pursued by hissing seas, we sheered away from those cliffs.

'Thank God!' Mr Belloc cried. 'My children, my children! Thank God! Well done, my children, we would have been drowned. I didn't think it could be done. Thank God. Thank God!'

No sooner had the shout of hurray died on the air than another kind of shout was heard. It came from Aitken and A. D. Peters who seemed to be wringing their hands, writhing in pain, pressing their thumbs into their palms and holding their hands out towards me with questioning and angry looks. Had they really been expected to hang on to that rope, they asked? It had torn the skin off the palms and fingers of both hands and blood was dripping on the deck. They were in agonizing pain. It was my fault. I felt awful. I should have known it was more than human hands could do to hold a mainsheet in a gybe like that, even four hands together. I gave the tiller to Peter Belloc at once and went to look closer and then to get some dressings. Saying one is sorry for hurting someone is no balm for severe pain. I felt very much reproached. Only gradually as their pain lessened was I able to say, admitting my fault repeatedly, how terribly sorry I was. But their pain continued for hours and it was not until next day, when healing had begun, that they more or less forgave me.

It was a stiff following breeze now and we should have reefed the mainsail, but as we had never done this and two of the crew could not use their hands it was a lesser problem to stagger on, overcanvassed though we were, till we reached Durlston Head. The *Jersey* handled very steadily. The sun shone on our backs and we rushed along, the emergency was over and all except poor Bill and A. D. Peters felt jubilant. Mr Belloc began to sing.

Suddenly someone said 'Look!' and pointed astern. We all turned and saw our dinghy, the huge jolly-boat, charging down on us on the back of an approaching wave. It was half full of water and came at us at great speed, slewed to the side of and past us and was then brutally tugged straight by the rope that held it. As the wave passed the rope tightened like a bar while the *Jersey*, rushing with the next wave, tore onwards dragging the dinghy along at five or six knots with half a ton of water in it. We could not get it alongside and bail it out; conditions were much too rough. We tried a longer rope, but its surf-riding and charging became even more violent. We tried a shorter rope but then it struck the *Jersey* a blow on her rump and seemed likely to break up. We sailed on hoping for the best. Then came another cry of 'Look!' The rope had snapped and that gigantic dinghy was receding into the distance, riding the seas quite comfortably, even though waterlogged, now she was left in peace.

'Shall we go for it, Sir?' we all cried. 'No, no, certainly not, it's not possible. Damn!' Mr Belloc said. He looked angry and depressed. We knew he was thinking of the loss and the expense. He may have been thinking of how he had once lost a good serviceable boat that he had been towing behind the *Nona* while running before steep following seas in Bardsey Sound. There was hope that the dinghy might be saved by some fisherman with a motor boat, but even then there would be salvage money to pay.

Without this drag the *Jersey* went leaping along. Had this waterlogged 15-foot boat been responsible for her failure to come about? Partly no doubt; but the main reason could now be deduced from the behaviour of our jib. When the wind, coming slightly from the starboard side now, filled the headsails the jib blew out ahead in a graceful arc from mast head to bowsprit tip, as one sees in old pictures of ships flying before the wind or in distress or wrecked with one sail left. When we had been sailing with the wind ahead the jib must have sagged to leeward and in the moment of coming about become a bag of wind acting as a brake. Fancy not noticing it till now! We found that the jib purchase was 'chock-a-block', so we slackened the purchase tackle right off and took up the slack with the jib halyard. When that was made fast we could then get a good taut jib by hauling down again on the purchase. From that moment on, although I cannot say she never missed stays again, the *Jersey* went about much better.

From Durlston Head back into Poole Harbour and up to the quay was a three-hour sail with a fresh wind broad on the beam and little sea because the wind was now offshore. Mr Belloc still sat slouched and silent on the cabin top. He seemed tired by what had happened, the uncertainties we were discovering about handling this boat, the loss of the dinghy and the very narrow escape from shipwreck. It had been a strenuous day. His stamina was by no means exhausted, however, and he revived as in smooth water we came up past Brownsea Island, the *Jersey* now showing a fine ability to sail close to the wind. I was steering this bit of the course and I still remember the exhilaration of it: her beautiful clear expanse of deck slanting and levelling as she heeled to the gusts and buoyantly stiffened up again. There is nothing so good as the steering of a big boat with a tiller. A wheel may be less tiring because the strain is geared down by a system of cogwheels, but it is for this very reason less sensitive. With a tiller you know exactly what the rudder is doing and can feel the pressure on it. The response of the vessel to every movement you make is immediate.

After letting go in the yacht anchorage, which is some way out to the west of the town quay, we hailed a motor boat and asked the helmsman (or does one say 'driver'?) to take a message to Mr Shutler that Mr Belloc had returned *sans* dinghy and that he and four men wanted to be taken ashore. In due course a motor boat arrived and when we were landed at the quay Mr Belloc found that Shutler had already provided another dinghy which was moored further along. We all went to identify it so as to be sure of finding it after dark. It was exactly the same as the first; another gigantic rowing boat! Just as well perhaps, for five men in a small boat, in a high wind on a dark night, can sometimes all be drowned, even in harbour.

In the bar of the Dolphin with pints of beer the Old Man's spirits rose as if he was in his youth again, and the day's adventures were gone over with roars of laughter. We sat around a table. Presently there was placed upon it a dish with twenty fried eggs and other plates piled with bacon, bread and cheese. More beer came and then a bottle or two of port.

> Shall we turn to the breezier Belloc?
> No, no, leave it.
> (Stevie Smith)

Why leave it? Because so much of the irony he turned on to everything – the rich, politicians, bureaucrats, harbour masters (one of his favourite targets) – and often himself – was in the expressiveness of his manner, his voice, his own amusement; and when described, no matter how well, or reported verbatim this somehow comes out flat, banal or hearty. That is why, even if I could quote him exactly and describe the scene of the old hilarious Belloc and the young men in the Dolphin, I would say like Stevie Smith 'leave it' – it can't be done.

At ten o'clock when we got outside it was black, wet and gusty in the streets of Poole, and on arriving rather tipsily at the quayside we found a strong wind and very choppy water. It was going to be a hard row of about a quarter of a mile dead into the wind to get to the *Jersey*. The big new rowing boat was a blessing for safety and dryness but it was heavy to row. Peters declared that his hands were all right for rowing and so he and Peter Belloc sat on the middle thwart with an oar apiece. I sat in the bows and Bill Aitken and Mr Belloc in the stern. Out in the open water the wind was much fiercer. The oarsmen pulled frantically but made no progress. They got out of step with each other; if one weakened, the strength of the other turned the boat and the wind blew her off course. Mr Belloc shouted to one or the other in turn to pull harder to get the boat straight again. 'Now you, Peters! Peters! Now Peter, you Peter!' The wind blurred the distinction, confusion increased, we lost more ground. He took to shouting 'Peter Belloc, Peter Belloc!' But the difficulty of getting this boat along continued. I asked to be allowed to take an oar. After the success of the gybe at Anvil Point, something in my swollen head was telling me I could show them how. We lost more ground in the change-over with Peters and when I did get my stroke in time with Peter Belloc I found I couldn't match him. I may have had less beer at the Dolphin but I was weaker in the back. My failure decided Mr Belloc to abandon the attempt. The wind took but a minute to blow us back to the quayside and there, I don't know how, someone found a chap with a motor boat. We got into this and the huge dinghy was towed behind, which was less ignominious than being towed sitting in it.

Exhausted, we turned in to our bunks and dealt with the drips from the deck above by draping an oilskin or lying to one side of the wet patch. Mr Belloc lay down on his large rubber mattress with many groans and sighs. He took off his coat but nothing else, not even his boots, and covered himself rather clumsily with a blanket. His sighs became high-pitched gasping sounds, interspersed with 'my children, my children!' Others may have fallen asleep quickly but I could not. The noises of an anchored ship become very loud when there is no sleep and no talking or work to do. Things clanked and knocked and the rigging howled. In the small hours Mr Belloc's high-pitched sighs began again, very unhappy, suffering sounds. In an instant Peter was by his berth and asking 'What is it, Papa!' 'I can't sleep, my dear, I'm cold.' 'Yes, yes, Papa, I'll see to it.' Peter covered him with a lot more blankets and tucked them warmly round him like a child, Mr Belloc saying all the time 'Thank you, thank you. Thank you, darling boy'.

### HINDSIGHT ON THE ANVIL POINT AFFAIR

An old long-keeled pilot cutter, with sails that were not actually made for her, might well have difficulty in coming about under some circumstances, such as in short, steep or confused seas, and it might depend rather a lot on good team work. But the slack jib was nobody's fault but our own and there we failed on a point of ordinary seamanship. The drag of the waterlogged dinghy was certainly a factor in the second missed stays, which put us in the predicament of having to gybe immediately because we were sailing into a sort of corner made by the cliffs at that part of the coastline.

When I had had more experience in handling the *Jersey*'s big gaff sail, I saw that the right thing to have done, the moment it was decided to gybe, was to lower the peak at the same time as putting the helm up. With the gaff horizontal and the sail billowing the *Jersey* would not have exerted that strong weather helm that made it so difficult to bear away. It is true that the swinging gaff at the moment of the gybe might have damaged its jaws or another part, but we would have turned and got away in a much smaller circle, even two or three boat lengths.

# ONE OF
# MR BELLOC'S CRONIES

M R Belloc, talking as we sailed along, was always referring
to old cruising companions of the *Nona* days who were
with him on this or that passage, exploit or mishap: Phil Ker-
shaw, John Phillimore, Edmund 'Bear' Warre. The only one of
them I actually met was Edmund Warre, a son of Dr E. Warre,
Head Master of Eton in the late nineteenth century. He was an
architect and a bachelor. He had a brother also nicknamed 'Bear'
and the two of them were known as White Bear and Brown Bear,
but of the latter little seems to be recorded, at any rate in
connection with sailing.

Soon after the Anvil Point affair, several of us who could now
count ourselves as Hilaire Belloc's second-generation crew were
invited to lunch at the Arundel Hotel, which was off the Strand in
Arundel Street and from its other side looked down on Temple
Place, with a fine view of the Thames and the Victoria Embank-
ment. It was at that time a place where you might often see
high-ranking members of the Roman Catholic prelacy or dis-
tinguished-looking ecclesiastical figures. The impression of it
that remains in my mind is of red carpets, white table-cloths
reaching to the floor and black boots protruding from soutanes.
Occasionally the black boot protruded from purple silk. One
might sometimes see someone kiss the ring of one of these

eminences. Mr Belloc did not do this, but once in the salon where we were gathering he darted forward and gave a rather hasty, though deeply respectful, bow to a purple dignitary who had just entered the room. The lunch was not noisy for the atmosphere was slightly subdued, but it lasted well into the afternoon. It looked like coming to an end when Mr Belloc announced 'And now we'll go round and harry the Bear!' In due course a taxi containing Mr Belloc, A. D. Peters, W. N. Roughead and Jim Hall (the two last well known to Mr Belloc and to join us on future cruises) and myself drew up at a door in some secluded Mayfair street or square – it could have been Little Stanhope Street – and in we went. Leaving us in the hall, Mr Belloc shuffled down the long passage of the apartment, calling out 'Bear! Where is the Bear?' The Bear was found in one of the rooms, doing nothing in particular it seemed, though possibly drawing. It was about half-past three or four o'clock. I was curious to meet someone, whose name I had so often heard, of the generation connected with the cruises of the *Nona*. Our intrusion, and an intrusion I am sure it was, into a life of regularity, ease and decorum was accepted with amusement and Bear's welcome was most genuine.

A decanter of sherry appeared in no time and very fine dry stuff it was. It was long after his lunch, but we were still in a very expansive after-luncheon mood, a state with which Bear could hardly have been in tune but he didn't show it. While Mr Belloc told him the story of our escape from shipwreck on the Dorset coast, Bear Warre sat there smiling, at ease, impeccably dressed in a check suit of perfect cut and a silk scarf and open collar. He was the epitome of the English gentleman and tremendously handsome; indeed a beautiful man, with his steel grey hair (no baldness), substantial eyebrows and curling moustache, firm jaw, straight back, blue eyes and, as yet another gift from the gods, a rich and manly voice. His nickname seemed odd: it suited Belloc better.

He did not say much, and I was a little disappointed; but there was a gap of about thirty years between him and the youngest of us.

I met him a year later at one of those London season balls, drinking champagne after the supper; immaculate, suave, handsome as ever, and I listened again to the fine musical voice. He said he was planning a cruise that summer. 'With Mr Belloc?' I asked, rather incredulously. 'Oh no! I'm chartering a yacht with a friend, just us two and a paid crew, you know, a skipper and a boy.' I was disappointed in the Bear once again. I thought for a moment of Mr Belloc, the Old Man roughing it with young men in his ramshackle boat, with nothing to bolster him up against the fatigue, the wet and the cold except wine and his hip-flask of brandy. And then I visualized these two middle-aged gentlemen, Bear Warre and his friend, doing things in nineteenth-century style, with a compartment between the crew and themselves below decks and with probably nothing to do above decks except steer and navigate. And of course, at my age, then about twenty, I was disdainful of it. But gradually, as my own middle age approached, I came round to understanding their point of view. That is how gentlemen sailed in the nineteenth century and the Bear was still in the nineteenth century. If you are middle-aged and can afford it, it is not to be despised as a way of getting to sea. I have often imagined Bear Warre and his companion in a fast, well-found yacht, steering and navigating from the cockpit while the crew reefs sails or shakes out reefs, sets a topsail to order or lowers it. Then, anchoring in some lovely harbour after a not too arduous passage, at supper in the saloon genially accepting through a hatchway the hot food prepared by the boy, with a bottle of claret, port to follow, cigars and talk well into the night; leaving it to the paid crew to worry about flapping halyards, the bumping dinghy, the proximity of other vessels, the anchor chain and all those things that get one up, underclad, in the hours of darkness, even in the safest of harbours.

But youth would have none of it and Hilaire Belloc, of course, would have none of it; quite apart from not being able to afford it. He would only sail with a crew he could call 'my children'.

# POOLE TO YARMOUTH
# AND A LIFEBOAT REBUFFED

SHOREHAM on the Sussex coast was Mr Belloc's 'home port'. The *Jersey* had been found in a creek of Chichester Harbour and sailed round to Poole. Now he wanted to have her under his eye in a harbour he had known most of his life and from which many of the cruises of the *Nona* had started. Sailing eastwards up the Channel is easier than going the other way, or tends to be; which is perhaps why he felt confident enough to sail from Poole with only two to help him, myself and Eric Clarke, a friend of mine. It was the summer of 1932, almost a year after the near disaster at Anvil Point.

With Eric I had discovered sailing and the sea and gained all experience I hitherto had of coastal waters, but only in small boats. Once again Mr Belloc came to my home to talk about the plans, to have a look at my friend, and brief us as to dates and even the times of trains to Poole. After he had gone Eric told me that he had felt quite frightened of the Old Man, but I reassured him.

Eric Clarke was a fellow medical student. We shared a small boat and made many exploratory voyages in it, from Norfolk to the Isle of Wight, from Yarmouth to Yarmouth! He was a good seaman with a lot of stamina when it came to long hours of sailing in hard conditions. He devoted the first half of his life to medicine, some middle years to farming and the rest to music and conducting orchestras. His love of the sea and the life one led upon it was profound. He kept a humorous detachment from most of the banter and heartiness that sometimes invades sailing boats and was rather reserved: a peaceful companion.

This year the *Jersey* had a new dinghy in place of the heavy 15-foot boats that Mr Shutler had supplied. It was a little 10-foot boat, which could be pulled up on deck when making a passage and stowed upright on the starboard side, where one could also sit in it, rather comfortably. It also had a small mast, sail and centreboard, which were often used in harbour. We were well pleased with this new acquisition as we set sail from the harbour and made for the sea on the first leg of our journey to Shoreham.

There is a shoal near the entrance to Poole Harbour, just to the east of the channel, which runs southwards from the narrows for about one mile; it is called Hook Sand. With a south-west wind a sailing boat leaving Poole should be able to keep to the channel and have no difficulty in clearing the sandbanks to leeward. With a wind more to the south than south-west there would be a need to tack.

The wind was south-west and we should have been able to hold a course due south long enough to get well clear of the shoals to leeward. But somehow, because of drifting sideways or the occasional puff of wind coming more from the south, we found we were getting too near them and would have to make a tack. She failed to come about. Once again, neglecting to get up the jib really taut was the factor finally responsible for her missing stays. I don't remember who was steering or who could be blamed, I only remember Mr Belloc shouting 'Back the jib', going forward with rapid little shuffling steps and seizing a boathook with which he then poked the jib out to port in the hope of the wind taking it aback and blowing her head round. It was no good. In a moment we were half sailing, half drifting eastwards. It was Anvil Point with the same decision to be made; try again or gybe? Was there room for either? The certainty that there wasn't room was brought home to us in a few moments by that strange feeling of disequilibrium as a boat is brought to a standstill on a sand shoal or mudbank. One is drunk for the space of a second and lurches forwards or backwards as the case may be. The sails were filled and the *Jersey* heeled slightly to the wind, but we were stuck and eddies and bubbles were flowing along the ship's side from stern to bows as the ebb tide now swirled past us. It was a falling tide and scrambling to get out the kedge anchor was summed up as hopeless by the Old Man and a waste of effort. So down came the sails and we sat on the cabin top to examine the picture in which we were now framed – a venerable old boat gone aground, in full view of the hotels and *plage* of Sandbanks on a fine sunny morning, with a gentle breeze and only wavelets slapping her sides; no swell and no bumping; a falling tide with about an hour's ebb to go and the certainty of floating off on the flood in about three hours time. A passing fisherman in a motor boat came over to within talking distance and made an agreement with Mr Belloc to come back at 2 p.m. when we should be floating again, and tow us into deep water.

After saying 'my children!' several times Mr Belloc went below, while Eric and I stowed the sails and walked the deck which sloped downwards from stern to bows like a ship running before a sea. There were no other boats to be seen either entering or coming out of Poole. There came the sound of a cork. Our mood of humiliation and despondency changed. What's a few hours on a sandbank on a sunny day? It's a waste of time, that's all. We might still have time for the passage to Yarmouth, Isle of Wight, in the afternoon. So, down the hatch we went. The Old Man filled our mugs with rich red wine and we all cheered up.

Suddenly, while we were eating our lunch, there came a shout. I darted up on deck and looked round to see where the hail had come from. I was very surprised to find there was a lifeboat a short way off, with full crew in yellow oilskins glistening in the sunshine, bobbing up and down and seemingly waiting there. At first I didn't connect it with the shout I had heard and while I was looking round in other directions the shout came again; it was from the lifeboat! So it had come out for us! I couldn't believe it. It began to draw near, and the man standing in the bows, who turned out to be the coxs'n, shouted that they had seen us run on the sands, knew the danger we were in and had put to sea at once to save us from shipwreck. The lifeboat would tow us off, he said, if he could come aboard and make fast a line. Fortunately I knew something about the laws of salvage at sea (see page 70), and saw a red light. The coxs'n was carrying a grapnel, a three-pronged hook, on the end of a rope which he held in one hand with the coil of the rope in the other. I explained that we were quite confident of getting off the sand without help in about two hours time and that we did *not* want a tow. But the lifeboat was now practically alongside, and the sturdy crew were smiling at us − or was it grinning? − and looking rather hot in their oilskins and sou'westers. To my great surprise and indignation the coxs'n ignored what I had said as if he had heard it incorrectly and simply threw the grapnel on to the deck of the *Jersey*. I leapt forward and threw it overboard, splash into the sea. At this rebuff, an angry roar of voices came from the lifeboat. Their benevolent smiles immediately turned to outrage. 'Do you know where you are?' they shouted, 'You're on Hook Sand! There's many a ship's been wrecked on this sand! You'll catch it. You'll be sorry for this. You'll learn. Wait and see what's coming to you. This is the dreaded Hook Sand. Silly fools!' and so on. Mr Belloc was now on deck and heard all this with astonishment. The three of us stood and watched the lifeboat sheer off and head for Poole, with the coxs'n and his crew in dudgeon.

When at about two o'clock the *Jersey* began to straighten up and lift slightly to the waves, sure enough, our man turned up. This time *we* gave *him* a rope to make fast and he very soon had us off the Hook and in the deeper water of Poole Bay. He came alongside to receive a fiver from Mr Belloc and thanks from all three of us. I hope his good act was not observed by any member of the lifeboat's crew who, that night at any rate, might have breathed revenge.

From Poole to Yarmouth is a bit under twenty miles. It was

now about mid afternoon and the wind had veered to the west and freshened; a perfect wind for this passage, coming on our starboard quarter, our backs to it instead of facing it and all sails pulling hard. As we got over towards the Isle of Wight, some sea got up and the movement made Mr Belloc slip and come down on deck rather heavily. He sat up and said he was all right, then rolled himself down to the lee scuppers (the space between the bulwarks and the outer edge of the deck – the place, incidentally, where they turned the hosepipe on the drunken sailor). There he remained for the next few hours, half lying, half sitting, propped on his elbow and looking over the bulwarks. 'Sir, won't you come and sit in the stern? It's very comfortable here.' 'No, my children. I'm quite all right, I'll stay here.' Presently a bigger sea sloshed aboard and the water ran along the deck, down to the lee side and out through the scuppers, having passed under Mr Belloc. 'Sir, are you sure you won't come aft where it's dry?' 'No, my dear, I don't mind, I'm better here, I don't want to move.' Nor did he move till we came to Yarmouth four hours later.

The approach to the Needles Channel is particularly grand when the late afternoon sun is blazing on the white cliffs of the island and on the Needles which are like the jagged teeth of some vast fossilized jawbone projecting out into the sea. The *Jersey* had been sailing at four or five knots all the way across Poole Bay and now the wind blew harder to give her five or six. It was just as well, for she would not otherwise have got through the channel from which the ebb tide was now pouring westwards with equal speed. The tremendous cliffs of Tennyson Down on our right and the Hurst lighthouse on our left were almost stationary and were there to be enjoyed for a very long time, if one could take one's mind off the tussle going on between sail-power and tide. If we had arrived with an east-going tide, which we would have done had we not been detained on Hook Sand, it would all have been over in a short glorious rush at a speed of twelve knots; seven for the ship and five for the tide. But now our speed against the land was sometimes zero, sometimes half a knot. In the narrows, the tide, which is pouring westwards at its fastest here, becomes a smooth sheet of water, broken only along the shinglebank where the lighthouse stands by a phalanx of stationary waves with foaming heads continually breaking and tumbling down their forward slopes. At times we hardly moved or even lost ground, but when a stronger gust came, giving the *Jersey* a speed of probably seven knots, we crept up. And so, seeming to climb up the back of one stationary wave, through the foaming crest and down the other side, we gradually got them all behind us. The *Jersey* was wonderful: with her long straight keel and deep draught, she held a steady course and was easy to steer, though hard on the helm, of course.

Reaching the wide waters of the Solent at last, where the tide was slacker, we made good speed over to Yarmouth and our mooring for the night.

Hilaire Belloc describes this particular passage in 'Armada Weather' in his collection of writings, *On Sailing the Sea*:

> The mighty river of salt water pouring through
> The narrows bethought itself of Tennyson and
> Ran quite silent, too full for sound or foam.

### THE POOLE LIFEBOAT AND THE LAWS OF SALVAGE

In my early youth, in about 1928, I had a half-decked boat which I bought at Burnham-on-Crouch and sailed right up the Thames to Cadogan Pier, Chelsea. She broke her mooring rope one night and was found bobbing about in the tideway off Battersea Park next day. A smart fellow who took people for joy rides in a speedboat got hold of her and towed her back to the pier. He stuck a notice on the mast with his name, claiming her as his property unless full salvage dues were paid. I was shocked, incredulous, furious and miserable all at once. I rushed and got information from *Brown's Nautical Almanac* about salvage at sea, and found that the salvager could indeed claim a minimum of one-third of the value of the vessel. I pleaded that this was a river but the speedboat man said he could claim it because the Thames was tidal water. In the end he took pity on me, seeing that I couldn't afford to pay without sacrificing a holiday, and let me off with a lesser sum. But it taught me a lesson. I then discovered that when there was no danger to life, lifeboats could claim salvage when they towed a ship off a shoal or out of the danger of running on to one, and this was rather a shock. I had always imagined that a regard for fellow men in danger was the principle of action, sometimes very heroic action, of the lifeboat crews and the Royal National Lifeboat Institution which, then as now, was supported entirely by voluntary contributions; but that they occasionally profited from the plight of stricken ships surprised me very much. In course of time, however, I have come to see that this game of salvage claims and bargaining, bluffing in the face of danger, though next door to piracy, is an acceptable part of life on the sea. The sea is rough and seafarers are tough, and from time to time mistakes or bad luck have to be paid for.

Not wishing to cast any aspersions on our admirable and valiant lifeboat crews, I sent the description of the incident with the Poole lifeboat to the Royal National Lifeboat Institution and received this comment on the affair from one of their staff:

> The RNLI as an organization never claims salvage. It exists solely for the purpose of saving life at sea and the public subscribes the funds it needs for this very reason.
>
> However, it is the legal right of anyone who saves or helps to save property at sea, to make a claim for property salvaged and thus RNLI crews are entitled to claim. If they do, however, they forfeit any payments that they would otherwise receive from the RNLI and have also to pay for the fuel consumed and put right, at their own expense, any damage to the lifeboat or its equipment.
>
> It is difficult to say, so long after the event, what were the intentions of the Poole lifeboat, but they had probably been called out by HM Coastguard because the yacht had been seen to be in trouble and were annoyed that they had left their jobs and launched at considerable expense to the Institution only to find that they were not required. They may also have been concerned that the yacht was in more danger than its master realized and would not have known that a fisherman had already been engaged to tow off Mr

Belloc and his crew. Indeed, one wonders what would have happened had not the fisherman returned – the situation may not have been so amusing.

Finally, in 1958 (as far back as our records go) there were 154 cases where salvage claims could have been made and only 22 were put forward. In 1983 there were over 1,000 cases where claims could have been made and none were put forward. I suggest that this reflects the unselfish attitude of the crews who give up their own time and risk their own lives in order to save people who find themselves in danger, often by their own carelessness or neglect.

The performance of our lifeboats, as given by the RNLI, is indeed impressive. These men are the admiration of all yachtsmen and the presence of the lifeboat stations along our coasts is a source of reassurance for which we are constantly grateful. I admit to having been oversuspicious about a salvage claim on that occasion. The Poole lifeboatmen, having come out as a duty and finding their help was not required, could rightly feel put out. There was something, however, about the way that grapnel was thrown and the high dudgeon in which they departed when it was rejected that made me feel they had come out for a little more than the response to a coastguard's signal. And why not? We were a sitting duck for a salvage claim: no danger to life, a temporary predicament, an easy tow and only a short distance from harbour.

If they were hoping for a salvage claim on unsuspecting yachtsmen, after towing the boat off the sand, I don't blame them. We dodged it; that was part of the game. But this incident occurred fifty years ago and, as the statement of the RNLI shows, such things are not in the minds of those who go out to yachts in trouble today. What a lot we owe them! I had not realized the extent of it.

# YARMOUTH,
# ISLE OF WIGHT

A S Yarmouth drew near we had to collect our thoughts about
a suitable place to drop anchor. To enter the little harbour
was out of the question. Today the forest of masts is so thick that
as you pass from midway out in the Solent Yarmouth looks like a
hairbrush on its back. But even in the 1930s there were too many
boats in there for a motorless monster like the *Jersey* to enter
under sail, with an Old Man and two boys in charge, even to go
alongside the wharf. So looking beyond the pier, where the little
paddle-steamer comes from Lymington, we searched for a bit of
room among the crowd of yachts that lay at anchor or on
mooring buoys, eastwards along the shore; white, pale blue,
dark blue, green, with varnished masts glinting in the evening
sun.

The correct approach, according to the book, for a yacht
wishing to pick up a mooring or drop anchor with wind behind it
and tide against it, would be to reduce sail till the speed of the
boat over the bottom equalled the speed of the contrary tide.
Then, when virtually stationary relative to the ground and other
yachts, let go the anchor, lower all sail and let the chain run out as
the tide carries her back for a suitable length. The wind was still
strong, our speed through the water was fast; so was the tide; it
would be tricky. Mr Belloc took the helm while Eric and I got the

mainsail down, which was a tussle with the wind behind us, hoping that with headsails alone she would still make way over the tide: she did. We crept up to a position that seemed clear of the many boats bobbing around us. Down staysail, down jib; she stopped; the tide took charge and with the first backward glide the anchor splashed down followed by 10 fathoms of chain. Then came the gratifying tug as the hook took hold. We had arrived and in a moment we too began to bob in the swell and the running tide. Mr Belloc seemed well pleased.

There is always a period of inertia just after a sailing boat comes to anchor in a strange harbour or home port. The sails are down and in heaps, the cordage slack, the chain tight and bubbles on the surface of the tide come flowing past; it is one of the best moments in sailing. In training ships, or racing yachts, yachts with paid crews or boats with disciplinarian skippers, some people on board display a burst of energy of a different kind to that required at sea, a house-proud fussiness about appearances, the rolling up of sails, tightening of rigging, coiling of ropes, even swabbing of decks or business with flags: those who do it, or are made to do it, miss one of life's precious moments, that of 'arrival inertia'. It is often at evening that it is most enjoyed. The window-panes of houses reflect the sun, the sky tells of the weather that is spent or what tomorrow's may be. If it is high tide the water brims up and laps the unwetted stone of quays and jetties, lights come on and make snaky reflections in the ripples. Someone has just the energy left to open a bottle of wine or twist the whisky cap. Someone may say we are too close to the fairway or to the shore and we shall probably have to move; but the mood is – 'don't let's bother with it now'.

We sat on the deck of the *Jersey* in this pleasant state and as we watched Yarmouth with its little thin church tower becoming silhouetted against the yellow sky, there appeared in the foreground a dinghy with one man in it sculling fast to make over the tide towards us. When he was within a few yards he announced, still rowing to keep level, that Mr (or it may have been Colonel) C. . . who lived in that house (pointing to one of several conspicuous houses on the high ground above the anchorage) said we were much too close to his moorings and would we please leave immediately. Mr Belloc gave a courteous apology for him to take back to the gentleman, gave his name, his illustrious name, and said we would do so as soon as we could. If it had been the harbour master who had sent the message, Mr Belloc would probably have stood his ground and sworn he would stay where he was at least till the next morning.

Arrival inertia had come abruptly to an end, so we rowed ashore and went straight to the Bugle, that charming old inn that stands on your left as you step off the pier into the street. Eric and I sat in the bar while Mr Belloc set off up the hill to find the house of Mr C. . . and pacify him. The innkeeper, a handsome swarthy man in blazer and grey flannels, told us he knew Mr Belloc of old, probably in the year when he wrote the short prose poem to Yarmouth which is to be found in *Hills and the Sea*. The innkeeper remarked rather disparagingly on the great change in him since his last visit there, fifteen to twenty years ago. To be sure, he had a round back, a biggish belly, a shuffling gait, a husky voice and other signs of ageing, whereas the landlord, who had of course aged by the same span of years, was, for a publican, a well-preserved man with no signs of corpulence and seemed proud of it. But what work had he done? What worries had he had? What did he know of the toils of the writer's trade? And if it was drink he had in mind, Mr Belloc had doubtless drunk vastly more wine than he had (no whisky or gin), but was the Old Man not at this moment walking up the hill at Yarmouth, after a day at sea in a fresh breeze? And, though we could not know it, he was to live to be nearly eighty-three. When Mr Belloc returned we had a meal, with beer, in a little dining parlour. It was rather alarming for us two young fellows, each still a literary ignoramus, to be dining with this Goliath of the literary world, but there were no silences; a question, especially on a historical subject, would set him off. The little parlour has been enlarged by the knocking down of a wall, but on a recent visit to Yarmouth I have sat in the Bugle in the same place as we sat fifty years ago.

He was pleased with the way he had mollified the angry gentleman on the hill. Mr C. . . turned out to be an admirer of Hilaire Belloc's writing. He was probably proud to have his mooring fouled by the great author. And Mr Belloc had given him then and there a signed copy of *The Cruise of the Nona*, which happily (or perhaps with an underthought of its usefulness in pacifying plaintiffs in harbours) he had with him when he came aboard at Poole.

After supper he looked at the wine list and, noting that there was some Madeira, ordered a bottle; it was excellent. When the landlord next appeared, he asked him how much he had in stock. There were only three bottles left, I think. Mr Belloc asked if he could buy them. The landlord agreed and he paid for them on the spot. There followed one of his pieces of 'Advice', well known to his friends for their sagacity or idiosyncrasy. 'My children, good Madeira is rare. Most of it is thin, acid stuff. When you find a good bottle like this, buy it. Buy the whole stock if they will sell it,' adding, as he often did, 'and if you can afford it.' He spent the night at the Bugle. The next day two new crew members, A. D. Peters and W. N. Roughead, were due to arrive at Ryde. I was to meet them and bring them to Yarmouth.

W. N. Roughead was a colleague of A. D. Peters in his literary agency and Mr Belloc knew him well in this capacity. He is said to have had several sides to his character, but one side of him sufficed for all of us on the *Jersey*, his bonhomie. He knew nothing about sailing when he first came aboard at Yarmouth, and the happiness he found in discovering it all in the cruises that followed radiated out of him and gave him a continual mild euphoria. He was the most active, industrious, cheerful and unselfish crew member of all the assortment of men who sailed with Hilaire Belloc in the 1930s. Roughead played rugby football for Scotland and had been captain of the Scottish XV in his youth. He was a bachelor, an extrovert possibly protecting a sensitive melancholy thread in his character, and he was of course a 'hearty', something the life of the ocean wave makes us all to some extent. Intellectuals and aesthetes on the whole don't take to it very much. But he was more discriminating in tastes and friendships than most so-called hearties are.

His courteousness and decorum seemed rather old-fashioned but were really just the traditional politeness and affability of the Edinburgh Scots. He had a light Scottish accent; the pure vowels, clear-cut consonants and slight lilt of the voice added to his charm. We all called him 'Rough' or 'Roughy'. His family or people belonging to other sides of his life called him Nick or Nichol.

There was something a little Boswellian about the way he spoke to Mr Belloc; the great respect his manner expressed and the often repeated 'Sir'. But Mr Belloc, though a Johnson-like figure, never said 'Sir' to him or to any of us, only to respect-worthy strangers. We were not in the eighteenth century, though at moments, if we had been in wigs and breeches and sitting in a tavern, with Roughead throwing questions at 'The Great Man', you might have thought we were.

I went to meet the new crewmen, taking the little Isle of Wight railway. The train arrived at Yarmouth from Freshwater Bay on its way to Cowes and thence to Ryde. It wound along steep hillsides, through thick woods and over rushing streams, giving fleeting views of small old country houses sheltering down in the quietest corners under woods that leaned and cowered from the winds above – a life left behind in the nineteenth century. Peters and Roughead were rather impatient with the timetable of the journey back to Yarmouth and decided on a taxi. The winding lanes took us closer to village life and the occasional sight of Isle of Wight people, but the journey had none of the magic of the train. At Yarmouth they walked about entranced by the forgotten world they had come to, then off to meet Mr Belloc aboard. We described our dramatic sail from Poole. It was mid afternoon and time to be off. We would show them how things were done.

As we wound the anchor up the work became harder and harder, the chain began slipping on the capstan and another turn round it was necessary. Though expecting every minute that the anchor would break out of the mud and come smoothly up, this never happened. We all peered over the bows. There was the anchor right up to the surface, but under its fluke was a big heavy chain stretched very tight forward and astern of us.

'My children, we *have* fouled his mooring!'

'No, Sir, we've fouled a dozen I'm afraid! It must be a ground-chain,' I said, 'and all those yachts ahead of us and behind us have got buoys attached to it.'

There followed a stream of curses from Mr Belloc, expressing frustration, worry about the expense, fear of possible action for damages, the certainty of a bill to pay and at the same time a sense of farce at holding a dozen rich men's yachts on the fluke of his anchor. In the hope that it would disengage itself, we let the anchor run to the bottom again. After a pause we set to on the capstan, but it was the same back-breaking grind and up came the ground-chain once more, firmly hooked by the fluke. This time we raised it almost to the surface and I managed, by crouching on the bobstay, to pass a loop of rope under the chain and up on to the deck. When this rope was made fast, we were able to lower away the anchor, swing it free and heave it up on deck. The *Jersey* was now holding by a short piece of rope the Yarmouth Harbour yacht-mooring ground-chain. The strain on that piece of rope was terrific. Its fastening had now jammed so tight that we could not undo it and decided to cut it instead. With the first stroke of the knife it parted with a bang and the *Jersey*'s bows rose with a jerk about two feet out of the water.

Once out in the tideway we hoisted our great tanned sails and as we sped eastwards I hoped that the picturesque departure of the old pilot cutter would erase the blot we had just made on the glossy face of the yachting world.

Mr C. . . , if watching with binoculars, cannot have been so pleased about Hilaire Belloc's visit after all. Ground-chains, not being elastic, have to be laid straight again at someone's expense. Whether Mr Belloc received a bill for our misdemeanour, I never heard. And although it was our joint decision to drop anchor where we did and the blame could be shared, I did not ask. I should have, but I am quite sure he would not have dreamt of letting the young men pay anything.

Yarmouth to Ryde was a pleasant sail of five hours or so, anchoring at evening off Ryde. Ryde is not a harbour, it is just a pier, but the town climbs on to high ground which shelters the anchorage from west winds. In the morning – it was Sunday – Mr Belloc went to Mass.

# MR BELLOC LIKED TO
# SHOCK NON-CATHOLICS
# (AND CATHOLICS TOO)

HE was rowed to the pier by Eric Clarke and then found his way to a Catholic church. He did not suggest to anyone that they should accompany him. He knew we were a pretty heathen lot.

From the unassailable fortress of his faith he seemed to like to startle people – throwing pebbles at them, so to speak – by talking irreverently about the forms, rituals and trappings of the Catholic Church; things having no sanctity in themselves for Catholics, but often imagined to have by non-Catholics. My father told me an anecdote which is characteristic of him. He and Hilaire Belloc were on a walking tour and one night shared a room at an inn. Hilaire snored so loudly and so continuously that my poor father hardly slept at all. Early in the morning, thoroughly refreshed by *his* night's sleep, Mr Belloc went off to Mass. He came back very pleased with the way he had timed it and added: 'And I lit a candle for you, Desmond, and I stuck it *r*ight under the nose of the idol.'

At Ryde, too, he was pleased with having hit off the right time for the actual celebration of the Mass, missing what were for him inessential, the preliminaries and sequels. Another thing he maintained was that swearing and blaspheming were no fun and no use for the unbelieving. Certainly when in a fit of mounting

D.M. opening a bottle of wine for Mr
Belloc.

Anvil Point: the moment of the gybe, as I
later depicted it.

Running before the wind after Anvil
Point and before the dinghy broke adrift.

The *Jersey* in Lyme Regis, with Mr Belloc on deck.

Right to left: Hilaire Belloc, Lord Stanley of Alderney, who came to sea in plus fours, walking shoes and a trilby hat, Peter Belloc and D.M.

Mr Belloc with a mug of wine.

Father and son.

'I see a rock, my children.'

With W.N. Roughead and D.M.

Ready to go ashore. Jim Hall is on the left.

frustration at the cussedness of some inanimate object or 'mechanical contrivance', a frequent occurrence when sailing, he suddenly shouted 'Christ!' – it was a shock to all of us and had a steadying effect on him. He got fun from irreverence in many little ways. In his early years of editing the *Tablet* he was often short of copy, he said, and particularly of news, that is news of special interest to Catholics. 'I would accept anything,' he liked to say, 'as long as it had the slightest Catholic flavour about it.' When asked for an example, he replied 'Well, NUN MEETS HIPPOPOTAMUS IN NARROW LANE – I would accept that.'

Men can become very bawdy at sea, in their cups. We were sometimes gloriously bawdy with Mr Belloc, as we drank his wine in the cabin of the *Jersey*. I have said that he could be blasphemous; he could be splendidly bawdy also, as bawdy as Rabelais – but he was never blasphemously bawdy.

# RYDE TO SHOREHAM

SHOREHAM, the *Jersey*'s destination from Poole, is some
thirty-seven sea miles from Ryde; a good day's sail. We set off
on the Monday. The most direct course lies close to Selsey Bill
and takes one through part of that complex field of shoals and
rocks lying between the Bill and the Owers, marked by a lightship
in those days, now by a buoy. Hilaire Belloc was fascinated by the
fact of the sea having only comparatively recently invaded this
large area of inhabited land. He has described it in *Hills and the
Sea* under the title 'The Looe Stream'. Thus:

> The sea began to eat up Selsey. Before the conquest – though I cannot
> remember exactly when – the whole town had gone and they had to
> remove the cathedral to Chichester. In Henry VIII's time there was
> still a park left, out of the old estates, a park with trees in it; but this
> also the sea has eaten up; and here it is that I come to the Looe Stream.
> The Looe Stream is a little dell that used to run through the park.

He imagines the finding of walls of Roman palaces and relics of
bronze, marble and mosaic under that shallow sea. And goes on:

> The tide coming up from the channel finds, rising straight out of the
> bottom of the sea, the shelf of this old land, and it has no avenue by
> which to pour through save this Looe Stream, which therefore
> bubbles and runs like a mill-race, though it is in the middle of the sea.

On the day of our passage to Shoreham he was full of it. The Looe Stream is well described in the *Channel Pilot*. Mr Belloc had an old edition of this sailor's Bible, which he loved and read for pleasure. I wish I knew the year of it. It was probably long out of date, but although revised editions were frequently brought out (there had been eleven since it was first published in 1856) he would have none of them. The sea, like Mr Belloc, is conservative and changes very slowly. He did not therefore expect buoys, whose positions had been thought out by mariners over a century or more, to disappear or change their stations from one year to the next. And, for his period of time at any rate, he was probably right; the marks, buoys, lights and lightships seemed as fixed as the heavenly bodies. I think he felt there was very little chance that he would meet with any disconcerting change and that he could navigate better by sticking to the old book he knew so well. He admired its style, saying it was good stuff all through. What I have read myself of old editions I have certainly found comprehensive, economically expressed, concise and clear as to the different kinds of danger to beware of.

He read to us aloud, from his old *Channel Pilot*, the directions for the Looe Stream. The following quotation is from *Channel Pilot* Part I, eleventh edition, 1920:

> *The Looe Channel*, lying as it does within the whole line of dangers, barred at its narrow western entrance by turbulent overfalls, and having in many parts not more than 16 feet at low water, is only adapted for vessels of light draught or for those possessing local knowledge, except under very favourable circumstances. Great judgment is requisite to avoid being caught within it by night, and no seaman should take this passage at any time unless with a good breeze and plenty of daylight before him, nor should a sailing vessel attempt it with an adverse tide.

This he thought an admirable piece of writing, which says all that is important with a great economy of words and comes near to poetry.

I remember no detail of the sail from Ryde to Shoreham nor of the passage through the Looe. It must have been undramatic, though a ghostly or uncanny atmosphere could easily be worked up on what has been submerged ('Hark! Was that the sound of a church bell we heard there just now? There is no bell buoy marked on the chart! There was a church there once'). A sense of the supernatural more easily pervades where the sea has devoured or can be seen to be devouring the land than where the opposite has taken place and the land has soaked up the sea; as at Pevensey where William the Conqueror entered from the Channel into a harbour large enough to contain his whole fleet. Where his ships floated then is now all cultivated land, or streets where no ghosts linger.

# BOULOGNE,
# CROSSING THE COLBART,
# CRÉCY, FOG

M Y next cruise in the *Jersey* took place about a year after the
sail from Poole to Shoreham, where the boat had spent the
following winter. It was 1933, I think, in late summer and
glorious weather. Mr Belloc very much wanted to cross over to
France in his boat which he had not yet done since he acquired
her. His plan was to start from Shoreham and 'creep up the coast,
eastwards' to Folkestone, where George Bowles was to join him,
and then make a crossing to Boulogne. After some discussion, we
made our way down to the south coast and assembled for what
promised to be a splendid expedition. Jim Hall, who was to sail
frequently with us from now on, made his first appearance on this
trip. The crew for the sail finally consisted of George Bowles,
A. D. Peters, W. N. Roughead, Jim Hall and myself.

It was said of Hilaire Belloc in E. C. Bentley's clerihew that 'He
seems to think nobody minds his books being all of different
kinds'. The same could be said about him as to his crews. Jim Hall
was a strange ingredient in the salad. His father was a Catholic, a
convert from the Anglican Church, and had a strong tie with Mr
Belloc on this account. Jim as a small boy had been an acolyte
serving Mass and later went to the Oratory School. All those links
had lapsed, however, in the course of his rampageous youth.

He was not quite a young man when he first appeared on board the *Jersey*, nearing thirty, but still had the tearing high spirits and exuberance of the schoolboy – an Oratory boy, treating everything as a lark and avoiding being serious if he possibly could. He was very good-looking, with a tall forehead, beaver-brown moustache, auburn hair (now thinning rather badly), dark brown eyes with concentrated gaze and a deep and charming voice. Even though he could produce his charm like an actor, for fun, and often did so with his tongue in his cheek and mocking amusement in his eyes, he was indeed a genuinely charming person, warm, responsive, humorous and kind. But because of so much vitality he was exhausting to be with for long and in drinking he was impossible to keep up with. He had been an ace driver in motor racing and beaten scores of records, and when we used to meet again on land between sailing episodes he took a wild delight in driving us in his car at racing speed down to remote pubs in the heart of Sussex, with our hair standing on end and calling for mercy.

But he was a welcome crew member because he was cheerful in bad times as well as in good and his sense of fun and sense of farce helped morale all round when things went wrong. Sailing, one could say, is one-third glorious, one-third monotonous or boring and one-third unpleasant, even hellish. There were some monotonous periods, as on all voyages, and with the lack of anything to feed his exuberance, Jim's spirits did slump and the exhaustion of his life as a whole seemed to show through; but not for long.

We cast off from the *Jersey*'s berth in late morning in pleasant light airs, but about an hour after leaving Shoreham it was rather suddenly decided to put into Newhaven, briefly, for Mr Belloc to visit the Post Office and send a telegram. We had to tie up to one of the pontoons that lie on the west side of the dredged channel opposite the passenger ferry boats and other shipping. It is a simple enough business even without a motor when you have had some practice, provided you have a fair wind from some direction. But sailing vessels have no brakes and the chief difficulty is in reducing sail power at the right moment, so that the boat will carry enough way to reach the pontoon or quay with not too much momentum; nor too slowly, in which case she would stop short, out of reach, looking foolish. Warps must be flung to any helper on the pontoon or a man must leap on to it with warp in hand as soon as near enough. Alas, we had had no practice at this and things went badly wrong. The harbour master happened to be there. He was another who recognized Hilaire Belloc of old. He did a lot of shouting. He shouted orders to us, the crew, and he had the impertinence to shout at our skipper: 'Now, Mr Belloc, look after your men!' The Old Man was furious and muttered to himself.

After we had at last been properly tied up, the harbour master became chatty and overfamiliar with those of us who were on the pontoon, talking about 'old Belloc', who had been in and out of Newhaven often enough in his earlier sailing days, and saying 'He's a "card" isn't he!' But, typical of the cheapness of the man, he did not have the courtesy to go on board and speak to him. Later, with food and wine, we had a good laugh over the 'shambles' of our arrival and docking at Newhaven. The Old Man began to revile all harbour masters again and ended with an aphorism: 'People of no education put in a position of absolute authority, invariably abuse it.'

The Seven Sisters, which rise up just to the east of the town, have many garbs and show many faces to the passing mariner according to the slant of the sun and the light in the sky. One of the things in favour of the Newhaven–Dieppe crossing to France is the splendid view of these cliffs one has on leaving or approaching the port.

As we left Newhaven later that afternoon, the sun was still high and shone from due west, cloudless, warm and still very bright but with that first touch of yellow that comes with its decline and the change to evening light. When we had got some way out, the full range of the Seven Sisters could be seen. What is England made of? It is made of chalk, of course, that is perfectly obvious; with a beautiful film of green on top. And here you see the land broken open as if to show you the composition of the rolling downs in this part of the country. Though chalk is soft and crumbling stuff, the sharp shadows cast by the sunlight that afternoon made the cliffs seem as if they had just been sheered off by the blow of a mason's chisel.

There is a rhythm in the undulation of those cliffs, a steep rise on the westward side and a gentle slope to the eastward, repeated seven times until your eye comes to Birling Gap and then begins the slow rise to Beachy Head, as far again as the run of the Seven Sisters but to three times the height. It was a calm and pleasant sail all that night, rounding Dungeness in the small hours and reaching Folkestone in the brightness of the morning. That afternoon, with Commander Bowles aboard, we set sail for Boulogne.

This could hardly be called a sail. There was practically no wind and what is more the *Jersey* had grown a lot of 'grass' on her bottom, which was a drag on her movement under light airs. Looking over the side you could see the green weed trailing through the water; it was thickest just below the surface. So long, however, as a breath of wind filled the sails and she maintained the momentum of her 19 tons we moved steadily at a speed of perhaps half to one knot. There was no swell, no effect upon the water by which any wind force could be judged, the Beaufort scale was therefore 0 or calm. But the sea, especially in the Channel, is never flat and there were undulations from all directions which imparted a gentle rolling movement to the hull, which swayed the mast, which shook the sails, which flapped and flapped and thereby fanned her along. This lasted from sunset, at about 8 p.m., for the next eight hours. And simply by pointing in the right direction, which there was just enough movement to do, we flapped our way across the English Channel. The motion was so gentle that a wine bottle standing upright on the cabin top needed no attention.

I put myself in charge of the navigation, which was reduced to the simple plan of sailing a course south-eastwards, allowing for the ebb tide to carry us southwards beyond the southern end of that shoal called by the French Le Colbart and by the English The

Ridge. And having cleared it, the same course, if we could still sail it, would bring us to Boulogne. It would be a surprising thought to most people, gazing across the English Channel from the cliffs of Dover or Folkestone towards the French coast, that there is a part of the sea about half-way across where you could touch the bottom with a long oar; but so it is.

No watches were set. I went to my bunk for a doze from time to time, but kept popping up on deck to see if the course was still sailable or flappable and conditions were steady, though actually one can tell this better from the bunk than from on deck. One is 'woken by the new life in the hull and the run of the sea along the sides' (*The Cruise of the Nona*). It was a wonderful night, warm, almost windless and slightly hazy, but with stars visible overhead. The impression of this passage that I retain is that Mr Belloc and one or two companions spent the entire night, from sunset to dawn, talking. Whenever I came up for navigation purposes, there they were, a little group, on the after deck, one of them steering, or perhaps I should say keeping the ship pointing in the direction of France. It is rare for such gentle and balmy conditions at sea to last so long.

But there was the little matter of Le Colbart half-way over. It seemed as if, sailing on our present course, the ebb tide was not going to carry us southwards far enough to clear the south end of the shoal. As we were now approaching it, judging by the position of the light buoy just visible at the end of the shoal, we would cut across it somewhere near its south end. It was about midnight. I began to take soundings with the lead. The little group went on talking and laughing. Five fathoms (thirty feet)! A shallow sounding for mid Channel. There was supposed to be at least six feet over the shoal at low-water spring tides, and it was now near low water. The *Jersey* drew six feet. Though falling, the tide would still give an added depth of a few feet. So even if we were heading for the shallowest part, we would clear it if we held on. Another sounding, three fathoms; the bottom was rising steeply. Five minutes later two fathoms. From now on, I kept sounding almost continuously and at last after another ten

minutes or so the depths increased again. We were over. I went to
Mr Belloc and said 'Sir! We have just crossed the Colbart.'

The *Channel Pilot* of 1938 (Part II, North Western and
Northern Coasts of France, page 338) reads as follows:

> The Ridge or Le Colbart is a dangerous steep-to shoal, which, with
> depths of from 1¾ to 10 fathoms over it, extends about 9½ miles
> North Eastwards from a position about 13 miles West-North-
> Westward of Cap d'Alprech. The sea breaks heavily on this shoal,
> especially with the wind against the tidal stream. Vessels should
> never cross The Ridge even at high water.

Now Mr Belloc's copy of the *Channel Pilot* was a much older
edition, as I have mentioned earlier in connection with the Looe
Stream. He knew the passage about Le Colbart well and was
particularly delighted to quote it now:

> *no vessel should ever attempt to cross it under any circumstances.*
> (*Channel Pilot*, Part I eighth edition, 1893)

I think he said 'no *mariner*' should ever attempt to cross it, for he
was particularly fond of that word. So there were circumstances
when it *was* possible and the old *Jersey* had done it. He was
delighted; authority had been flouted. And whenever his
thoughts chanced to return to the matter that night or next day,
out came the quotation again.

Dawn at sea is more often dull and grey than anything dramatic. There comes a moment when you cannot say it is lighter but
you can see people's faces slightly better. Mr Belloc's face looked
puckered like a child who has just woken up; he rubbed his hand
up and down over his face, treating his nose as if it were
gutta-percha, gave a great yawn and went below. A more definite
breeze began to blow, producing on the surface not wavelets to
catch the light, there being as yet no light, but a million little
shadows that danced on the backs of the dying swell. I too went
below. We could still hold the course. Someone took the helm
and by eight o'clock we were looking out for Boulogne.

Landfalls may be sudden because you have not been looking out for land for some time or looking in the wrong direction, or, as on this day, slow and subtle. Land is at first just imagined: then some infinitesimal change whispers it might be true. Look away, leave it; the temptation returns to look again. Something blue-grey on the horizon has slightly deepened. Dismissing it, you look for similar tones along the skyline west or east of it, to prove to yourself that this is what all horizons look like at that time of day, with that angle of the sun's rays. But then, with the lapse of a little more time and due probably more to a change in the clarity of the atmosphere than to the distance the boat has travelled towards the haven, there comes conviction – it *is* the coast, it is Boulogne.

Mr Belloc had not been across the Channel by sail, and in his own boat, for many years. He had, of course, crossed over often 'by machine*ry*,' as he called it, 'in a packed and bullied herd'. This arrival, with a fair wind, after the calm and dream-like passage we had had, put him in the highest spirits. Not wanting to get in among the fishing boats of Boulogne, we turned in to the *avant port*, which is a tidal basin on the south side of the harbour. In the southern corner of this we dropped anchor and by means of the dinghy ran a stern line to the quay. No sooner had we done so than the joys of arrival inertia, so pleasant in a foreign port, were interrupted by the presence of a man on the quay looking hard at the *Jersey*. He was obviously not the harbour master, nor was he even uniformed, unless an old peaked cap can pass for a badge of some sort of officialdom. The *Jersey* was not flying the red ensign, I do not think she had one. But hearing our conversation, he concluded we were English and that, even though we would not understand French, we would nevertheless have to be ordered about. He shouted something about our being 'mal mouillé là'.

Like a man-of-war suddenly opening fire, Mr Belloc thundered at him across the water in French, so volubly we could not tell whether it was the language of a gentleman or that which he had learnt in the French Artillery in his youth. The official staggered, but answered back and got another and then another burst of fire from the Old Man. The argument continued furiously for quite a time while we nudged each other and enjoyed the sport. Then the man slouched off, talking to himself. The *Jersey* stayed where she was.

It was a lovely day. Mr Belloc decided to take us to see the battlefield of Crécy and to lunch at Montreuil. Montreuil is about thirty kilometres from Boulogne and Crécy-en-Ponthieu is about the same again. It would be an expensive taxi drive with five of us. Roughead suggested that we all subscribed something towards it. He discreetly collected our contributions and when we were ashore, getting the Old Man alone for a moment and using his great charm and tact, persuaded him to accept it. Hilaire Belloc would never have asked for such a thing himself but his generosity frequently exceeded his purse. He had been fairly well off for only a few years, from about 1910 to 1920, and now always had money worries, so he was grateful. But there was still the lunch at Montreuil; that was entirely at his expense. He would not share it, saying something like 'I could never have crossed the sea and got here without you, my children.'

When we got to Montreuil he halted the taxi at the inn and arranged for some food to be prepared for our return, then we drove on to Crécy. Here Mr Belloc directed the driver out of the village on to the road to Wadicourt. About one kilometre along he stopped him and we all got out and followed Belloc the historian into the fields.

> I know not what that fascination is which attaches to seeing, touching, standing on the very site of some great business of the past. I cannot analyse its nature, but I feel the strength of it profoundly.
>
> (*The Cruise of the Nona*)

And he imparted some of the strength of it to us on this occasion, as on many others.

The battle took place at this time of year (26 August 1346), he said. It was now midday, but we must imagine it evening. We were standing in a field of sugar beet. The roots were big and we could step over them without doing harm and so advance till the ground began to fall away in a gentle slope to the south. Mr Belloc said that this was about where Edward III placed himself, in the centre of all his troops, looking into this shallow bowl of country, which was and still is called the Val au Clercs, though it was not deep enough to call itself a valley. He went on in this manner:

The Black Prince, only a boy, was at the head of his right flank. Although there is sugar beet as far as we can see, at the time of the battle there must have been open heath and there was said to be soft ground at the bottom of the slope. It was not a marsh, but from the exaggerated accounts written of knights floundering in it you would think they had ridden into a bog. There had been a very great thunderstorm during the afternoon with pouring rain, which may have made matters rather worse for the horses; but what the heavy going did was to prolong the time the knights were exposed to the terrible arrows of the Welsh bowmen. The Welsh bowmen gave Edward a unique strategic weapon. Their 6-foot bows were very powerful. Their arrows were 3 feet long and could penetrate chain armour and bring down horses or throw them into panic. Their range was 350 yards. The bowmen had years of training, and were for that reason very valuable men. They could stop a cavalry charge, which nothing else could do at that time. But they had to shoot fast and concentrate all their power in a few minutes. If they failed to stop the charge or ran out of arrows they could be set upon and were done for. The battle of Crécy was won by this weapon. When the arrows came with such concentration and such force no one could stand up to it.

The French knights came on in their hundreds, with no organiza-tion. The aim of each one was simply to find another knight, knock him off his horse, bring him down, not kill him, but capture him alive and demand his ransom.[1]

---

[1] Of the longbow, Sir Ralph Payne Gallway, in *The Crossbow* (Holland Press: London, 1958), observed: 'Whatever its extreme range may have been (350–400 yards) there is small reason to doubt that at a distance of 150 yards the old English longbow quite equalled, if it was not indeed superior to, the flintlock musket or "Brown Bess", which was carried by our soldiers till about 1840.'

In skilled hands, the longbow could discharge six shafts per minute, whereas the crossbow and musket could manage only one – and the longbow was more accurate than the musket. If 120 bowmen had faced 120 musketeers at Crécy, victory for the archers would have been easy. English archery with the longbow, in fact, was a very peculiar gift of God.

One could imagine the horses plunging and rearing down there and the Welsh bowmen in ranks stretched out among the sugar beets to right and to left of us, a bit further down the slope than where we stood, but still high enough to be shooting downwards into that stampede. One could imagine the armour, the unhorsed knights, the blind King of Bohemia, wall-eyed, groping in the mêlée and mortally pierced by an arrow. General J. F. C. Fuller states the rout began when the Welsh bowmen fell upon the knights and killed them with their long knives, then robbed them of their valuables – much to the annoyance of Edward III, for a dead man fetched no ransom.[1] I do not think Mr Belloc mentioned this. If he did, I am sure I would have remembered it because of the irony with which he would have told of Edward's anger.

Now back to Montreuil. The talk continued in the packed taxi and turned, I don't know how, to Richard I, whereupon Mr Belloc made one of his memorable remarks. 'Very few people realize that this great national hero they called "Richard Cœur de Lion" was simply a bullet-headed Frenchman, covered with pimples and probably a bugger!'

The hotel at Montreuil was none other than that made famous by Laurence Sterne in *A Sentimental Journey*; since identified as the Hôtel de la Cour de France. It was where he spent his second night in France and somewhat experimentally hired a manservant, the indomitable young optimist, La Fleur. The *auberge* still stands at the corner of the Grande Place. The main road from Boulogne to Abbeville crosses the 'Place' along one side and coming to the hotel turns sharply round it, downhill and out of the town. We did not drive in, but got out and walked through the high *porte-cochère* into the cobbled courtyard round which the old timbered house was built. There was a large awning of creepers on one side, a *tonnelle*, under which a table was set in welcome shade, while the sun blazed in the stillness of the yard. There was no one about. The place did not appear to be functioning as a hotel any more. I do not remember the lunch as being

---

[1] In *The Decisive Battles of the Western World* (Paladin: London, 1970).

hilarious, the Old Man was tired, but it was delightful. Here we were in the eighteenth century; Sterne had slept here. That morning we had been in the fourteenth century; Edward III had stood where we stood. And we would end the day, after a sleepy drive to Boulogne, in an old pilot cutter that belonged to the nineteenth century. Short of sleep the night before, we were aching for a siesta aboard. It had been the sort of calm and trouble-free night when plenty of sleep can be had by all, but we had spent it talking under the stars, and in crossing the Colbart.

On the way back from Boulogne to Dover, late the following day, we ran into fog and had a night of worry. We proceeded northwards with only a faint breeze and little steerage way; in the same manner, in fact, as we had come over, but with a great difference as to peace of mind, for then we had reasonably good visibility and now we were swallowed up in fog.

Hilaire Belloc described this particular crossing in *On Sailing the Sea*, published in 1939, in the chapter entitled 'Channel Fog'. It is a masterly description of the feelings of general unease or worse that fog at sea evokes and the way sailors are put out by this. It is well worth rereading or obtaining the book for this alone. Characteristically he begins by expressing

> a sombre pleasure in remarking those disagreeables which the false efforts of our time [the 1930s] cannot pretend to have surmounted; there is a sombre pleasure in recognising the persistent power of fog at sea. What is more, fog is a greater enemy than ever it was. Other things which men have done in their frustrated efforts to obtain happiness through mechanism have given sea fog greater powers and terrors than it had in the past.

Since fog is associated with calm weather, ships under sail in the days before steam were not going at any speed and collision, if it could not be avoided, was not so serious.

> But today [he continues] with dense capricious Channel fogs especially, the sea becomes in one moment a field of terrors, and the nearer you are to the Straits or to one of those headlands round which the main traffic swings, the more anxious the strain.

'Ah, but we have radar now,' people may say, 'and ships are regimented into east-going and west-going lanes'; but how much comfort does the modern yachtsman feel when contemplating the small square radar reflector suspended in his back-stay, especially when fog is compounded with darkness? No, if Hilaire Belloc were alive today, he could still have his sombre amusement at the helplessness of mechanized man when fog descends.

We had two frights on that night passage. The first was when a cross-Channel steamer loomed up right ahead and very close. Mr Belloc, who was up in the bows, actually ran with shuffling, stuttering steps towards the stern shouting to me 'Port your helm, boy! Port your helm!' She passed us red to red some thirty or forty yards away and going dangerously fast. The second Mr Belloc describes in his essay as a 'well-bred ship':

> A well-bred ship . . . at any rate she had the perfect manners of the sea and was feeling her way down Channel without haste and with due regard for others. As her great bows passed by us we saw a man on watch looking over, but all that fore-part of her was swallowed up long before her full length had gone by, so dense was the brume. We drew breath after a second salvation.

Hilaire Belloc's account of that crossing in 'Channel Fog' ends with our arrival at Dover the next morning. And here the delightful and kindly George Bowles departed for London, leaving the sound of his explosive laughter in our ears and his enormous enamel basin for washing as an incongruous memento of his brief sojourn on the *Jersey*; also a piece of 'jingle' which it gave him particular pleasure to quote. I do not know the author of this; it may have been Bowles or Belloc or another:

> The lion is a fearful beast
> From whom you flee in vain,
> For while you run with all your might
> He runs with all his mane.

We discovered on the voyage that Bowles was an accomplished amateur of the guitar. I had a cheap guitar on board for my own amusement, which had steel strings. This horrified him when I produced it, but he took it from my hands, tuned it very professionally and proceeded to play a Chopin mazurka (about ten bars of it, anyhow) followed by a chain of guffaws and exclamations that the guitar was the most *beautiful* instrument! He taught me many things about playing and told us much about the wonders of the school of classical guitar players in Spain; little known or talked about in England at that time, other than the emergent, immortal Segovia.

He did not come sailing in the *Jersey* again, which was sad, but he invited all of us to visit him in London any day, after five, in Bedford Street, at the offices of *The Lady*, of which periodical he was the editor. We often went. There was always a loud welcome. 'Ah, my dear MacCarthy! Come in, come in! My dear Roughead! Come in!' There was always sherry and he kept at his office one or two instruments from his fine collection of Spanish guitars. On these he would play after much persuasion, just to show their lovely tones, never getting to the end of a piece because of the laughter that seized him.

But to return to our berth in Dover Harbour. Mr Belloc wanted to get the *Jersey* back to Shoreham for the winter, so we set out later that morning for a down-Channel sail. There must have been a big anticyclone prevailing, a word he always objected to as being simply 'mumbo-jumbo' for fine weather. There was not much wind and what little we had from the east in the morning gave out at Folkestone in the afternoon. Instead of entering Folkestone Harbour, to lie among fishing boats and taking the ground at low water, we drifted westward with the tide until opposite Sandgate. Sandgate seemed to be then to Folkestone what Hove is to Brighton; the one thinking itself a cut above the other; a place for residents rather than trippers, standing on a range of high cliffs from which its ugly hotels of dark brick, with a green copper dome or two and white conservatories, looked down on a wide shingly beach. It is curious that on the French coast just to the west of Calais there is a place called Sangatte, a mirror image as it were, for all I know adopting the same airs about Calais as Sandgate about Folkestone. A mile or two to the west was Hythe, whose lifeboat, we little knew, we were to become acquainted with as a friend in need.

Letting go the anchor by Sandgate we swung with the tide, parallel to and about 200 yards off the beach. Not a breath of wind, the heat was baking, the deck almost too hot to stand on barefoot. Mr Belloc sat on the cabin top all in black, with mug of wine in hand, cap off and grizzled head, while we went over the side for a cooling swim. One by one, trousers off, shirts pulled over heads, we dived or plopped or splashed into the sea. I was the last to go and as I did so I saw Mr Belloc smiling and heard him say, half to himself and half to us, 'You're a hairy lot, my children, a hairy lot!'

Later we put him ashore in the dinghy wearing a loose-fitting, thin, black alpaca suit that flapped in the breeze and moulded to the shape of his legs and body. The charming photograph of him by Jim Hall in *On Sailing the Sea*, standing on the beach, pipe in mouth adjusting his Kodak, marks this moment (see pages 112–13). He spent the afternoon writing letters and drinking coffee in one of those big hotels and then we took him aboard again. He wanted to rest and sleep or read while we young men rowed round into Folkestone Harbour to spend the evening in pubs.

When the time came to row back to the *Jersey*, the night was warm, breathless and black. We rowed along the Hythe shore but could not find the *Jersey* anywhere. Had the anchor dragged or the shackle parted? And was Mr Belloc alone and asleep, drifting somewhere out on the sea in the darkness? This was not such a frivolous thought as it sounds; after half an hour's search we really did think something had happened, till we chanced to catch sight of her mast against a light on the cliff. But even as we approached quite close her black hull was hard to see. There was no light aboard. At the sound of our climbing on deck Mr Belloc's head appeared in the hatchway.

'Aren't you very late, my children?'

'We couldn't find the ship, Sir. No riding light, Sir!'

'Really! No riding light? Good heavens! I've been asleep you see and I'm such a born sailor I forget to put up a riding light.'

His omission was hardly surprising for he was prejudiced against them. They had tried his patience in the past; in this he should have the sympathy of all yachtsmen, past and present. In *The Cruise of the Nona* he wrote:

> And as for your riding light, which so often has to do duty when all are asleep on board, see that it is sound and of capacity and filled. You can hardly have too large a one; not for the sake of the light, but for the sake of the number of hours it will burn. And this I say, never having possessed one in my whole cruising life which did not leak or blow out in a gale, or come crashing down on deck through insecure fastening, or in one way or another behave in a fashion true and consonant to the 'Nona' . . .

We then did put one up and lit the cabin lamp and prepared for the sleep of exhaustion, beer and sun.

The next morning, Mr Belloc said he had had to change his plans and must go back to London, leaving us to sail the *Jersey* to her home port, Shoreham. The crew, however, also had reasons for not being able to stay on and it was decided to leave her in Folkestone until we could next assemble for that short passage. Folkestone was a bad decision, Dover would have been better, but shortage of time and the continuation of these windless days determined it. The *Jersey* was put in charge of a longshoreman who was to look after her legs and pump her out. And there she lay at the end of that summer, in this shallow harbour, taking the ground at low tide and thus seriously straining her aged timbers and planking.

# THE AFFAIR OF
# THE HYTHE LIFEBOAT

IT was not till early October that we could reassemble for this last trip of the year and take the *Jersey* from Folkestone to Shoreham. Mr Belloc could not come but said he envied the glorious run we would have with the east wind that had been blowing for several days and seemed determined to continue. The crew consisted of Eric Clarke, Jim Hall, myself and one Burgoyne, from a wine-merchant family with connections in Australian burgundy, who Jim thought might be a helpful friend.

Coming down from London on a Saturday by afternoon train we found the *Jersey* afloat, without her legs, looking neglected and dirty, with cordage slack and flapping and a lot of water in the bilge. In haste to be off with this lovely east wind we enquired too little into the extent of her leaking, but simply pumped her out, paid the longshoreman, set the mains'l and sailed out of this wretched, unsuitable harbour. Close-hauled, we just cleared the pier of the cross-Channel steamers and set a course for Dungeness, a twelve-mile run. Shoreham was sixty-three sea miles to the west. We expected to sail this night and half the following day, or less or more, depending on whether the wind kept up or flagged.

The sun shone, the wind was fresh and right behind us, the sea moderate. The *Jersey*, however, seemed a bit sluggish and her speed was disappointing. About half-way across Hythe Bay, as I was going forward to secure something in the bows, I happened to glance down the hatch and saw a suitcase that seemed to be moving of its own free will. On returning aft I took a proper look and was appalled to see that it was in fact dancing about on a flood of water that covered the cabin floor about a foot deep. We pumped furiously for a quarter of an hour, two on the gut-stretcher and one on the rotary pump down below, during which time I was sick, partly from fear perhaps. I felt weak, despairing and exhausted and the amount of water still in the bilge convinced me that at the rate we were leaking we should sink before we got to Dungeness, or, if we did get round and turned into smoother water on the west side, that would be no place in which to get help. If she did sink, out here in the bay, and we managed to get into the dinghy, all four of us, what chance would we have of being rescued in a roughish sea five miles from the coast? I longed frantically to get near the land so that when she sank we could get to the beach in the dinghy or swim and save our lives. Beating back to Folkestone in this wind and sea would be quite impossible. On the other hand in the comparative shelter of Hythe Bay our pumping might at last become effective. At the moment we were a feeble lot. Jim Hall was being sick repeatedly, Burgoyne was white and only Eric Clarke had the strength of a man. I don't think the others saw our plight as seriously as I did, but perhaps my fear was infectious and brought to an end the discussion of the pros and cons of struggling on as we were. We made a right-angle turn and headed straight for the shore of Hythe Bay, only six or so miles from Dover.

When we anchored some 200 yards off the beach the sun was setting, the wind lessening and the sea calmer. After some food and drink we really put our backs into the pumping. Quite soon the 'tomato soup' began to flow over the deck, the welcome sign of reaching the depths of the bilge, where the rusty pig-iron ballast lay, and then at last came the empty suction noise – she was dry. We were all right – for the moment. Had we panicked for nothing? Another try at the pumps after . alf an hour showed that we had not. She was filling again quite fast.

At sunset a fishing boat, guessing we would not choose such an anchorage if we were not in some trouble, came alongside to enquire. The skipper happened to be the coxs'n of the Hythe lifeboat. He said the lifeboat was a new one and he was taking the crew out for a practice run next day, Sunday, and could give us a tow to Dover; not as a 'rescue' but as part of the day's exercise. There would therefore be no question of salvage, just a tow. This seemed a godsend. I still had some wrong notions in my head about lifeboats claiming salvage. We thanked him and the start was fixed for 8 a.m. Jim Hall, Burgoyne and I now went ashore to telephone to Mr Belloc, leaving Eric alone on board to pump out every half hour. I am not sure why poor Eric was left alone; possibly for no better reason than that we all had to telephone about something – but more probably because landing on the beach in the surf would be tricky for only one or two of us. Certainly Mr Belloc had to be told and it was Jim who was going to take the bull by the horns. Afterwards Eric said that his spirits had sunk very low as the grey dusk came on, listening to the moaning of the wind, the clank of the rigging and the sloshing of the bilge.

Jim returned from his telephone call in Hythe to say that the Old Man was furious. 'You've got a fairer wind than I've ever had in all my sailing days,' he had said. We ought to carry on even if we had to pump the whole way. Mr Belloc thought it mad to go back to Folkestone, let alone Dover. Perhaps it was. It sounded no more than a simple bit of endurance; sixty miles to go, a passage of fifteen to twenty hours and four men to pump in turn. Perhaps it was wrong to accept the tow. But we were in no mood to set off then and there at the fall of night, knowing that quite a big sea was running out in the Channel and it would be particularly rough round Dungeness. In the event we probably were right not to risk it, for it blew a gale from the east next day.

At eight o'clock the next morning the lifeboat arrived. The boats rolled heavily and bumped together as two men climbed aboard by the chains – the skipper, 'Buller' Grigg, and one of his oilskinned crew. One of our warps was passed to the lifeboat through the hawsepipe of the *Jersey* in readiness while we got up the anchor on the capstan and secured it aboard. The mainsail gaff and boom were lashed down on deck, the bowsprit housed and the tow began.

As often happens when a weather system develops which gives easterly winds, gale forces occur along the coast, especially round the great headlands. As soon as we were well off the land it was clear we had a gale against us and were in for a ten-mile slog to Dover right in the eye of the wind against steep head-on breaking seas. The lifeboat was to be put to the test. But the sun shone brilliantly out of a cloudless sky all day. When the sun shows itself in a gale or any ugly situation at sea it is the greatest morale booster that sailors know.

The *Jersey* leapt, plunged and rolled. You could not relax your handhold for a moment. Wet with spray, we lumbered on at three to four knots. It was good to feel the tug on that great towrope as every crest was surmounted. But then, about half-way between Folkestone and Dover, our warp parted. The *Jersey* soon stopped and began to wallow sideways in the troughs of the waves. Without a sail set it was impossible to keep her bows pointing up and the motion was too violent for anyone to dare to move. We could only crouch and cling. Awful crashing sounds came from things breaking loose below decks. Immediately the lifeboatmen retrieved the warp and manœuvred to a position off our weather bow. A line was then cast from the lifeboat right across the *Jersey*'s bows using a murderous club of a thing, consisting of a lump of lead the size of an orange, on the end of a stick to which a line was joined. Woe to anyone who should happen to be struck by it as it flew over the deck! Buller Grigg seized the line and in a moment was hauling it in, bringing a great warp from the lifeboat. This he turned round the bitts of the old windlass and then round the base of the mast. On we went. The pump had to be kept going all the way and it only occasionally sucked dry.

We had a fair tide, but tide against wind always makes the seas seem steeper. When at last we reached the entrance to Dover Harbour the seas were tremendous and with the confusion always created by the 'backscend', where a big wall juts out into the sea, they became tumultuous. As the lifeboat turned in round the western arm of the mole she held the bows of the *Jersey* steady while the tide swung us slowly round until we were pointing fairly and squarely for the entrance, broadside on to the waves. It was the most dramatic moment I had ever experienced on the sea. The *Jersey*'s great black hull rolled her topsides to the scuppers from side to side and we leapt from glorious heights to awesome depths, shouldering off great lumps of sea which came from all directions. Then the final pull. With the cable straight as a bar and the wake of the lifeboat foaming from the power of her engines we moved fast between the two great stone walls of Dover Harbour and suddenly – there was peace. Inside the Harbour there was still a strong wind and a big swell, but it felt like utter calm. Had I been scared? No. I was absorbed in watching a fine piece of seamanship. Had the *Jersey* been in danger of foundering? Not a bit, she loved it.

Making over to a quay near Granville Dock, we tied up one behind the other. Out of the wind and in the sun it was hot and we peeled off our outer garments. Buller Grigg and his crew removed only their sou-westers. Although the quay was difficult of access from the town, a crowd started to gather while we were still congratulating the lifeboatmen and talking to them in their boat, for they showed no inclination to come aboard the *Jersey* and simply sat there as if waiting to turn round and put to sea again, which in fact they soon did.

Inevitably the press, like condors dropping from the sky down to a kill sighted with their telescopic eyes, appeared on the quay and asked to come aboard, or perhaps just stepped on to our private decks with notebook in hand. What they subsequently wrote soured the good relationship between the two crews.

When these reporters discovered, by questioning anyone in the area, whether in tarpaulins or 'flannel bags', that we had not been rescued from shipwreck but simply towed as part of a sea exercise of the new Hythe lifeboat, they wrote a muddled version of what had happened which appeared under the headline COMEDY

RESCUE. This mortified the men of the lifeboat, for whom the exploit of towing a heavy pilot cutter ten miles in the face of a gale had been no comedy. The coxs'n wrote to Jim Hall, who had been our spokesman with the lifeboat from beginning to end, saying that his men blamed us for this travesty of a sea story, due to the things we must have said to the reporters. Jim said there was malice in the reporting, stemming from local politics or jealousy between the citizens of Dover and Hythe. A few days later, as soon as possible after getting home, he went down from London to Hythe to try to lift Buller Grigg and his crew from their dudgeon. His enormous charm, aided by beer all round, was bound to assuage their bitterness, we felt. He returned depressed. They were practically all teetotallers or, at least, not interested in an invitation to a drink and a talk in a pub. Most of them were good Chapel-goers, too, and led abstemious lives. Such were the men who manned our lifeboats. But the coxs'n was friendly and understood that we were not to blame for the local paper's sneering report.

To end the story – soon afterwards the *Jersey* was moored in a corner of the Western Docks, where at low tide there is a patch of hard ground. With her legs fitted she settled upright on this and a shipwright came and examined her. There was a gap between two planks in her port quarter, her left buttock one might say, a foot below the water line. It was about two feet long and as wide as a letter box in the middle part. Pending proper repairs he put a 'tingle' over it. This nice word means a patch of copper plating. The hole is first packed tight with oakum. Then a piece of felt, shaped to cover amply the length and width of the gap, is placed over it, this is coated with bitumen and the copper plate placed on top and tacked down with copper nails closely set all round the edge.

The ship then spent the winter in Granville Dock, looked after by a very old sailor called Faringdon; a humorous character, a tiny little man, as deaf as a post, for which his two large cabbage ears were no compensation. He looked up at you with his hand cupping one ear and a smile of expectancy but probably heard nothing. His blackheads were enormous and he could drink a pint of beer by pouring it down his throat as one would if pouring it away.

# MR BELLOC'S VIEWS ON
# ERRORS OF NAVIGATION

M R Belloc liked to lend the *Jersey* to friends he could trust. It always amazed me how ready he was to do this, without any conditions or strict instructions and without any insurance as far as I know. This generosity gave me some of the most delightful sailing of my youth and as temporary skipper I could invite able-bodied sailors among my friends to join me, not all of whom he knew.

One of Hilaire Belloc's friends to whom he lent the boat was Alan Phipps, Lieutenant RN, son of Sir Eric Phipps, the Ambassador, who was plenipotentiary in Vienna at the time. Alan was an officer in destroyers in the mid 1930s. His destroyer was sunk in a naval battle in Greek waters in 1942, and he was killed soon after in commando action on the island of Leros. He was still in his twenties, a charming, gay and vigorous young man, with a cork-like buoyancy on life's troubled seas.

Although a professional sailor, he confessed that navigation was not his forte and thought it a great joke that on a night passage in the *Jersey* he found he had for some time been sailing up the north coast of France thinking he was sailing down the south coast of England!

As to the apparent absurdity of this and other navigational howlers, which form some of the stock jokes of all the sailing fraternity, Hilaire Belloc had several comments to make and these are to be found in *The Cruise of the Nona*. To begin with, he says that 'it is a thing that happens very much oftener than sailing men are willing to admit'. According to Belloc, the commonest mistakes are made in identifying a piece of land from the sea.

It is not only a matter of what is called today 'visibility'; though it is true that the thickness of the air makes a great difference to one's judgment of distance. No matter what the conditions, the most absurd mistakes can be made, and are made continually, and that by practised men. It was only the other day that I mistook Gris-Nez for the end of the cliff some miles to the east of it above the flat of Calais [probably Blanc-Nez].

A man who has been knocking about the Channel at night, and does not quite know where he is, except that he is somewhere off the Sussex coast, may (it sounds absurd, but it is true) take Fairlight in a haze for Beachy Head.

Much more excusable, and yet much more common than mistaking the outline of hills, or a headland, is the mistaking of a light. All of them have carefully marked spaces of time, a flash for so many seconds, or a change of colour, or what not. But a man cannot always be bothered to time these things, and in a little boat under a strain he may not be able to do so. But the very commonest form of error in this, as in everything else, comes from an absolute and false certitude. You say to yourself, 'There is no doubt at all that that light is such and such a light.' You have been waiting to pick it up, and when you pick up a light you are certain it is that light, unless the timing of it is quite grossly different from what you expected. But you may be quite wildly wrong. I suppose no one will believe me when I tell them that I have known St Catherine's (Isle of Wight) mistaken for The Hogue [Cap de la Hague].

He then refers to the mistake that could be made in his day, on account of there being two lighthouses on Dungeness, the new one on the extremity of the ness and an old one now further inland since the sandy point has gradually grown out into the sea. He goes on:

The worst mistake of this sort I myself ever made was mistaking the Varne Buoy for the South Goodwin Lightship. It is not so impossible as it sounds. The weather was thick; I had been drifting for many hours without much wind, and with no certitude of where I was except that I was somewhere in the Straits. I looked up-weather, to the north-east, and saw in the brume what looked like a hull and a pole. I could not be quite certain whether there was a ball on the pole or not, but I certainly took it for a lightship; and, judging from the time that I had left the French harbour, and the sort of pace I thought I had made in my little boat, and tricked by the weather (which was much thicker than it looked) I made sure that this apparently distant object was the Goodwin. It was not till I came within a hail of it that I knew it for what it was – the Varne Buoy, not a hundredth the size of a lightship.

How did Belloc navigate? How good was he, or how bad? He did not have a patent log in the *Jersey*, though the types that trail astern were common in yachts at the time and had been available since the turn of the century. I doubt very much that he had had one in the *Nona*. Even though he writes 'when she is doing seven knots she is doing well, and when she is doing nine she is excited' and 'when you are on a long passage, even with steady weather, you had better bank on three to four knots and no more', there is no hint of a reading from a log. He disliked what he called 'the craze for measurable things' and he would probably have put the patent log in that large category of things he called 'contraptions'. The compass, chart, parallel rulers, dividers, the lead and the *Channel Pilot* were all he wanted. The echo sounder, which at the turn of a nob and a reference to the chart can sometimes tell you in mist or fog that you cannot possibly be where you think you are, was not yet available to yachts. Even if it had been he would certainly have mistrusted it.

Not to know where you are fairly accurately in a yacht, at any moment, is looked upon disapprovingly now. Mr Belloc would have thought this absurd. He had 'local knowledge' all the way up the English Channel, which he delighted in; but which he had to admit sometimes failed him. The photographs between pages 80 and 81 show him navigating coastwise, in his own way, with binoculars, pince-nez on ribbon, and a chart and mug of wine to hand.

Had the new buoyage system been introduced in the 1930s, his last sailing years, we would no doubt have heard some fine invective against it at first, though he might straight away have thought the revised flash timing good. Personally, and here I seem to be treading in the footsteps of the Old Man, I am not yet convinced that the new shapes and colours of buoys have lessened our difficulties very much. That marvellous instrument the human eye can detect the merest smut of an opacity on the sea at great distance and the main thing required of a buoy is that it should have buoy-like characteristics and not easily be confused with any other UFO (unidentified floating object). The new buoys with their metal skeletons and yellow and black markings and the substitution on some of green colouring for black, do not seem to me to be identifiable with any greater confidence than the cones, cans and spheres of the old days.

# THE *JERSEY* DISMASTED
# IN MID CHANNEL

ALTHOUGH Alan Phipps made fun of his occasional errors of navigation, it was no fault of his seamanship that he was dismasted in mid Channel. After the affair of the Hythe lifeboat, the *Jersey* had spent the winter months in Dover under the eye of old Faringdon. The following year, as the weather improved with the coming of summer, Alan and a few friends borrowed her from Mr Belloc and set out for a cruise. I was not with them.

The *Jersey* was sailing westward, close-hauled against a moderate westerly wind, on a bright sunny morning, about half-way between Dover and Dungeness, when suddenly the mast broke high up at a point just below the jaws of the gaff. Everything crashed over the starboard side into the sea. The hoops of the mainsail slid down the stump of the mast, but the gaff and the bulk of the mainsail went into the sea. The boom hit the deck heavily and smashed the starboard bulwarks and stern-works. The jib and the stays'l, having no support from aloft, also went over the side into the water. The port-side shrouds strad-dled the deck – and in this plight she wallowed. Luckily no one was hurt. Alan said that they were all so completely taken aback that they just burst out laughing. To cut the story short, when they had got over their perhaps hysterical laughter they managed to drag everything back on board and it was not long before a coaster approached and gave them a tow to Dover.

But one more shock was in store for them. The coaster cast them a warp, a pretty heavy sort of thing I imagine, and they made it fast, not on to the windlass, but round the capstan on to which it was easy to throw several turns or equally promptly cast them off. The coaster headed for Dover, the warp took the strain, the *Jersey* followed. Now the power of the engines of even a small merchant ship is many times greater than that of, say, a trawler or motor boat that might have come to the rescue, and whatever speed that coaster made, the weight of the boat she was towing would not have been very noticeable. Was she in a hurry? We do not know, but suddenly, as Alan related, with a bang like a cannon shot the capstan snapped off at its base, hurtled over the bows and plunged into the sea!

The *Jersey* arrived at Dover at a gentler speed, with the towrope round her windlass. When the news reached him later, Mr Belloc said he would certainly have a new mast fitted but a new capstan, no. We would have to put up with the ancient windlass, and just what we did have to put up with is described on page 41.

So the *Jersey* was back in the hands of old Faringdon in Granville Dock. I found time to go down to Dover on Mr Belloc's behalf and see the shipwrights whom Faringdon had asked to assess the damage and put some timber on display for the choice of a new mast. The *Jersey*'s old mast, conceivably dating from 1846, had a copper sheath over the upper two feet of it below the hounds to protect the wood from the friction of the jaws of the gaff. It was under this copper that rot had been going on, for heaven knows how long. There were several great timbers on display in the shipwright's yard. They all looked far too big to my eye, because they were square in section from end to end, but I was told I would not think so when the spar was shaved down to round section. This was done by hand, with an adze. And they were right, when the new mast was finally in place it did not look too thick or too heavy, though it was decidedly thicker than the

Jim Hall steering and feeling low.

Some of Mr Belloc's crew at the helm: W.N.
Roughead (above), Eric Clarke (left) and
D.M. (right).

Mr Belloc on the beach at Sandgate, in light clothes for the heat.
Photograph by Jim Hall.

Barges at Pin Mill. The *Jersey* is lying just off the end of the hard, to the stern of the second barge.

The converted Aldeburgh fishing boat in which Eric Clarke and I gradually discovered the ways of the sea in 1929.

Mr Belloc, Roughead, D.M. and Eric Clarke, with a fair wind.

old one. As to cost, the figure of £14 or possibly £24 sticks in my memory for the spar itself. It seemed extraordinarily little even at the time for such a fine piece of timber. I do not know what the cost of shaving down the spar and stepping and rerigging the mast amounted to (the bill went to Mr Belloc) but it would probably astonish us by comparison with labour and material costs in shipyards, let alone yacht outfitters' yards, today.

The next time I sailed the *Jersey*, a few months later, it was to take her from Dover to Pin Mill in Suffolk where I knew the barge shipwright, Ted Webb, who would do the repairs to the smashed bulwarks and counter quite cheaply. It did one good to contemplate this newly shaped reddish tree trunk of a mast, but there was always the underthought – what, in a boat of this age, is going to go next?

A salvage claim by the company owning the ship which towed Alan Phipps to Dover was to be feared. I went on Mr Belloc's behalf to their offices somewhere in the streets of London's dockland. I was received into a wood-panelled room with a counter at one end covered with papers, behind which stood a burly figure who looked as if he had been a seaman himself. He welcomed me in genially and said that he had already written to Mr Belloc. The conversation went something like this:

'Who is this Hilaire Belloc? He's a writer, isn't he, a well-known writer? He's got plenty of money, hasn't he?'

'No! No! No! Far from it,' I said. 'He certainly is a famous writer and has written about the sea a lot, but it doesn't follow he's got plenty of money. Good heavens no! No, he's not at all well off. And the boat – although she's called "Yacht" *Jersey*, she's no yacht, as the captain of your ship will agree. She's been "in the trade", in fact, a pilot cutter, and must be ninety years old. Mr Belloc can hardly afford the upkeep such as it is and if he had a big salvage claim to pay he would have to get rid of her. That would be a great pity.'

'Well,' the burly man replied, 'I know; but I think our seamen ought to get something – that's all I'm thinking about. I'll write to Mr Belloc again and we'll settle for something; not much.'

I never discovered the sum finally agreed but I felt sure from the good nature of this man that it would not be a blow to Mr Belloc, who wrote me this letter about the affair:

## SOME OF H.B.'S MISPLACED INVECTIVE

King's Land
Shipley
Horsham
22 Oct 1936

My dear Dermod,

That is very good of you, to have gone to see those people. I was afraid that the old salt would regard me as a wealthy man! The simple souls go by whether they have seen a name in the paper, or again, by titles. They are always surprised when an unknown man dies worth a hundred and thirty seven thousand pounds odd. You have done nobly; tell me how much it comes to. But certainly nothing like what we feared. I am glad also that the Dover shark is coming down to 5/6 a week.[1] As they do nothing whatever but look at the boat and spit, nothing a week would be enough for them. At the end of the War there was a man who charged me a pound a week; and there is a gang of sharks called the Cruising Association which compels you to pay enormous sums simply for tying up an old dinghy. I am glad to say that the demands of the unlaborious are slowly killing the goose that laid the golden eggs. They will all starve soon – but I shall be dead and eating a a stuff called Ambrosia.

Always yours
H.B.

[1] This was old Faringdon, minding the *Jersey* at Dover, in Granville Dock, where she leaked very badly. This caused him to write a letter to Jim Hall beginning 'Sir, I can't keep pumping day and night . . .' He was no shark, and nor were the Cruising Association, but Mr Belloc called all longshoremen sharks indiscriminately, as a few undoubtedly were.

# AN OVERHAUL
# AT PIN MILL

WHILE at Pin Mill in the autumn of that year, after the deck structures and sternworks had been repaired by the shipwright Ted Webb, the source of leakage was gone into once again. The *Jersey* was brought up to the hard on a high tide and allowed to settle on her side. She lay at an angle of 45 degrees. The copper sheathing was fully exposed and examined down to the keel. The next day she was laid on her other side and the sheathing and planking inspected likewise by Ted.

When the *Jersey* was being fitted out in 1931, Hilaire Belloc had said that he no longer trusted any craftsman in Sussex. Perhaps he had had a disagreement with a local shipyard. If that was true about the craftsmen of Sussex, what a contrast was Ted Webb of Suffolk! Although under contract to the owners of local Thames barges, he found spare time to work on the 'famous hulk' as Hilaire Belloc called her. Ted loved this old ship and admired the strength and workmanship of her construction. After recaulking a few seams and replacing one or two doubtful bits of planking, cutting out a piece and inlaying new wood with the precision of a cabinet-maker, he declared that removal of all her copper sheathing in search of other trouble underneath it was very speculative and that you couldn't put it back if you found nothing. So in the end we left it. He renewed the counter, however, which had been smashed by the dismasting.

During all this refitting I lived aboard, resorting for comforts to the local pub, the Butt and Oyster. Living in the *Jersey* was rather primitive, but the only really unpleasant period was when she was on her side at 45 degrees to the perpendicular. For the first night, one could put up with the inconvenience of having to

Fig. 11. Living aboard at an angle of 45 degrees.
1. Obeying the laws of gravity, how it felt.
2. As the eye saw it (rotate the page 45 degrees to the right).
The resulting conflict was nauseating.

arrange a special seat to sit on and put the table at an angle so that things would not slide off, but one's eye was accustomed to the look of the cabin as composed of horizontals and perpendiculars and the force of gravity streaming through obliquely caused the lamp to hang at 45 degrees and clothes on hooks to hang right away from the hull as if on a merry-go-round. The table had to be adjusted to allow jugs and glasses to stand on it but even then the beer lay at an angle in its tankard, so that if you were on the 'down' side it flowed towards your mouth and spilt over, or if you were on the 'up' side it would not come to your lips. Another disconcerting thing was that a cylindrical biscuit tin placed on a board tilted upwards at one end *appeared* to roll up hill because the tilt was not in fact up to the horizontal level, but still slightly downward. All this set up strange stresses in the eyes and the sense of equilibrium. The labyrinth mechanism of the inner ear seemed not to like it at all. It could not be called motion sickness, but it became almost as disturbing. I could not contemplate a second night aboard and dived instead into a feather bed at the Butt and Oyster.

It occurred to me at this time that the well-known remedy or *pis aller* for old boats, of filling the bottom with cement, might be the very thing to give the *Jersey* a new lease of leak-free life. So I took up several planks of the cabin floor and set about the heavy and messy task of getting enough internal ballast out to get a clear view of the keelson and garboards and see what space there was to put cement in. I only had to get out three or four of the great iron pigs to see that she was already full of it!

When the *Jersey* put to sea again she did seem to leak less, but leak she did and in heavy weather badly.

# THE *JERSEY* ON
# THE EAST COAST

MR Belloc had been happy about the departure of the *Jersey* from her native waters of the English Channel to one of the sand-locked harbours of the east coast provided she was safe and, above all, would not cost him more than in one of the south-coast ports. After all, he knew the east coast from pre-*Nona* days and had written an account of a passage round Orford Ness ('The North Sea', in *Hills and the Sea*) in a strong wind, with a brute of a boat, on whose deck he afterwards poured wine as an offering of thanks. In 'The Sea Wall of the Wash', in the same book, he describes the imperceptible demarcation of land and sea where 'the sand and the mud commingle'. The next year, I introduced him to Pin Mill on the River Orwell, where he had never been. He had proposed a short sail. Pin Mill was an out of the way place in those days. It was and still is an anchorage – one can hardly call it a harbour – frequented by small yachts and Thames barges. It lies in a curve of the southern bank of the River Orwell, that wide tidal river which runs from Harwich Harbour inland some fifteen miles to Ipswich. Surprisingly, large ships now pass up and down, dwarfing the yachts as they shave past them.

Its many inconveniences had saved Pin Mill from becoming a smart and crowded resort of 'the rich'. Mr Belloc liked it for that and for its barges. The chief drawback for the city man who wants to step from a stone pier in neat clothes and walking shoes, either aboard his yacht moored alongside or into a dinghy or launch which will take him out to it, is that from half ebb tide to half flood the expanse of mud at Pin Mill is very wide. The rise, and fall, is 12 feet, and the jetty or hard runs with an imperceptible downward slope of about 12 feet in 200 yards. A dinghy moored to the outer end of the jetty at low water will be out of reach, even by wading, at half flood. One moored to the inner end of the jetty at high tide will be left high and dry by half ebb and would have to be dragged down 100 yards to reach the water. But by one means or another and a little foresight, frequenters of Pin Mill manage to get out to their boats on their moorings without too much mud on their boots. And with a bit of calculation they can row in for a drink at the Butt and Oyster, and row away again on the same tide without wading or having to shove the dinghy. The big yachts are now provided with all the conveniences they require at the marina a mile up river and their passing, but not stopping at, Pin Mill adds to the beauty of the scene.

Pin Mill is particularly beautiful viewed from the tideway. Big oak trees crowd close to the semicircle of foreshore, becoming very dark and shady as the sun falls behind them in the evening. A little street runs down to the centre of the bay. The Butt and Oyster stands at the end of it, right on the edge of the flats, jutting out so that at high tide it is lapped by the waves on two sides. But even today, the feature which impresses most, either when arriving by the road or coming ashore from the bay, is the magnificent Thames barges beached on the flats. Pin Mill has for perhaps two centuries been a place where these huge, extraordinary craft have come for a refit. When empty they can be floated far up on to the hard part of the flats where they remain high and dry except for a short time at the top of high water and where they are scrubbed and tarred and repainted, worked on by shipwrights and refitted by chandlers. These huge black hulls tower over you as you land from your dinghy, their great sprits and topmasts soar into the sky and on their champagne-glass counters you read their names, names with a history, family names, such as *Pearl, Two Boys, George and Arthur, Phoenician, Felix, Ironsides.*

## THAMES BARGES

In the 1930s, when I was exploring the sea in a small boat (a 19-foot Aldeburgh sprat boat, decked in and made into a little cabin cruiser with a cutter rig) with my friend and fellow medical student Eric Clarke, barges were to be seen all over the Thames Estuary and along the Essex and Suffolk coasts, even down Channel. They still had work to do. They were a friendly and comforting presence for the small boat for whom, even in these shallow waters the choppy seas, strong spring tides and lonely stretches, marked only by beacons, buoys and a few lightships, could be daunting at times. You could follow a barge in fog or misty weather if you correctly guessed where they were going. They always sailed with a fair tide. If a barge was anchored out at sea you knew it was waiting for a foul tide to slacken. They were recognizable at sea ten miles or more away by their tall tower of sail and you might sometimes see them when looking inland from the coast, sailing among cornfields and elm trees, creeping up a river to some inland village with a mill. Barges seemed always to be loaded down to the gunwale. They were stiff and heeled little when close-hauled or reaching, but if you came close up to one out in the Thames Estuary, its vast sails towering above you, the lee rail would be under and half the deck awash, the water rushing along it like a river. They were every bit as extraordinary as the junks of the Yangtze, which are a sort of counterpart to the barge evolved the other side of the world.

I learnt the art of seafaring while exploring the Thames Estuary and east coast from the Nore to Norfolk, occasionally single-handed. Barges, although their trade was declining, were still the dominant sailing craft. It all belonged to them. They had evolved the perfect rig, the perfect shape and the perfect technique of carrying cargo over shallow seas and into tidal estuaries. One's feelings towards them began with astonishment, which turned to curiosity, then admiration, fascination and gradually a sort of love for them. They were doomed like the dinosaurs, but not to total extinction, because the Thames Barge Preservation Society (which came to an end, sad to say, some thirty years ago) bought and saved a number of them and even today they are still refitted at Pin Mill.

I was at Pin Mill for a week before the date of Mr Belloc's proposed sail, living aboard and doing some fitting out. I began by scraping the mast. Hauling myself up in a bos'n's chair, I plied the scraper in one hand, holding on to the rope with the other and clinging to the mast with my legs. It was a slow and exhausting business. While I was up there a barge, sailing up to Ipswich, on the tide, came close enough for the skipper to shout 'What yer doin' up there? I can't see the part ye've done!' Peeved by this I came down and looked up; sure enough the part I had scraped was still almost as grey as the rest of the mast. I flung the scraper away. Evidently to scrape a mast from a bos'n's chair requires not only a very sharp scraper, but the use of two hands, all the abdominal muscles, the legs and the strength of a gorilla. I gave it up.

Having previously obtained Mr Belloc's permission, I painted the top of the mast from truck to shoulders light grey, likewise the gaff, the reefing end of the boom and the outer end of the bowsprit, in the manner of French fishing boats. I thought she looked very business-like and even more seaworthy than her ancient hull and rigging always suggested. There were many jobs to do; overhauling the running tackle, whipping ends of ropes, fitting new purchase tackles and an occasional splice to be made – all very enjoyable work because it was with rope and not with wire, which has replaced much of it now. It was, however, rather a lonely week and the sail-maker of Pin Mill, Mr Powell, who had recently remarried in his sixties, reading my expression over a beer in the Butt and Oyster, said, in his Suffolk singsong, 'I wonder you don't catch yer death o'cold – sleepin' alone!'

The peak halyard had to be replaced because the last one, having served for goodness knows how many years, had recently parted quite suddenly. We had been sailing with the wind aft. Suddenly the peak dropped down and disappeared behind the rest of the mainsail which, being still held up by the throat halyard, was converted into a sort of stumpy Bermuda rig. The surprise caused silence for a moment and in that silence there came another surprise; a sound like a game of ping-pong going on. The jaws of the gaff, now pointing to the sky instead of downwards, had stretched the cord on which the parrel balls were strung tight across the mast so that it parted and let loose a shower of these wooden beads, which bounced merrily all over the deck. Two surprises plus comic relief makes prolonged laughter and we were some time in getting on with the job of lowering the mainsail.

Mr Belloc with Roughead and A. D. Peters arrived in a taxi from Ipswich. It came down the steep little lane, right to the edge of the mud flats. Out got Roughead, Peters and then Hilaire Belloc. And there he stood in the evening sun all in black, an imposing but utterly incongruous figure on the rather squalid little strip of sand that edged the bay. Pin Mill had seen nothing so strange before nor has it since. After a few minutes gazing across the sheet of water that was slowly creeping over the mud and after failing to make out the *Jersey* far off on her mooring, he shuffled away and entered the Butt and Oyster, leaving a pile of baggage, books and wine to be put into the dinghy when at last the water came up to float it. This was to be a short sail for a couple of days, only as far as Lowestoft, and not a very happy one for Mr Belloc. He was not feeling well and his mood was affected partly by this and partly perhaps by the unfamiliarity of the east coast seascape and the absence of those nostalgic reminders of the *Nona* days which assailed him at every point along the Channel coasts of England and of France. Besides, the Essex and Suffolk coasts, though not featureless to those who know and love these grey waters, are comparatively dull.

When we got into the bar Mr Belloc had disappeared, but we ordered beer for all and then sat talking, drinking, waiting and eventually worrying. After a long time he shuffled in, sat down rather heavily with us and sighed. 'I can't rear, my children, I can't rear.' It was now evening. We decided to drop down the Orwell on the ebb tide and anchor out of the fairway near Shotley

Spit, a long tongue of mud that divides the Orwell from the River Stour. On our right as we went were cornfields and elm trees black against a violent red sunset. 'Red sky at night,' said everyone, except Mr Belloc who said 'Hot bath at night, shepherd's delight.'

It was the week of Harwich regatta, a yachting event which in the 1930s was becoming a greater and greater flop year by year. This year, however, four or five of the famous J Class yachts had dutifully turned up and were lying on moorings at the mouth of the Stour. We were due to pass Harwich in the morning on a fair tide going northward, before the racing started, but we thought we would have a look at them first. So we turned round the end of Shotley Spit up into the River Stour, sailing against the ebbing tide and therefore rather slowly. We got as near to them as we dared for our sail past. Close up, these yachts were astonishing things. The height of their masts was staggering and they seemed to be emitting a singing sound as the wind flowed through the elaborate system of stays and taut wires that held them vertical. They also made a honky-tonk noise from the flapping of the halyards against the mast, that hollow steel tube, like the sound of a blacksmith at his anvil or the Nibelung dwarfs hammering the gold under the Rhine. The clanking sound of a fleet of yachts at anchor is familiar nowadays, but it wasn't then. And the tinniness of it, coming from these queens of all the racing craft, was soul-destroying. A friend told me that when going about they made loud metallic sounds, the same sort of noise as someone rattling a bucket of cinders. For all that there was great beauty in their austerely designed hulls and the long sweep of their teak decks and their sky-seeking masts.

But it was now the *Jersey*'s turn to be admired. Close-hauled but with all her tanned sails well filled and drawing, 'aslant with trim tackle and shrouding', she crept past them over the tide, some thirty yards away. The professional crews of the J class were busy about the decks, scrubbing and polishing and did not stop to stare till one of them, an old skipper or bos'n, possibly a sailing master from Edwardian days, turned to us and burst out, '*There's* a fine old yacht for you! There's a fine old ship! That's what I like to see!' And we waved back to him; the skipper of a futuristic yacht looking nostalgically at the past.

Mr Belloc sang a great deal when at sea, on deck, especially when it was sunny and the *Jersey* was going along nicely with a fair wind. It was not a loud singing nor any kind of histrionic performance, as you might imagine from his 'old sea dog' appearance in photographs. No, he sang rather quietly, amusing himself on and on, mostly at tenor pitch. He had a very true ear. You might have wondered whether his voice was falsetto; it was not, but rather the way a good tenor sings who can send his voice up very high, softly and airily, more with his breath than his vocal cords. He did sometimes in a phrase or two let out his voice powerfully and clearly.

Most of the time his singing was just musing, like a blackbird on a branch. What came out was sometimes a song, sometimes bits of light verse. He was particularly fond of quoting W. S. Gilbert, but one wasn't always sure who it was. Some things seemed just to come out of his head:

> First we heard a scuffle
> Then we heard a shout
> And then we found Eliza
> With her entrails hanging out.

Then there were very old popular songs, such as:

> If it wasn't for the 'ahses in between
> We might gaze upon Her Majesty the Queen.
> We might see her in the Palace,
> Taking tea with Princess Alice,
> If it wasn't for the 'ahses in between,
> If it wasn't for the 'ahses in between.

And this extraordinary one, a marching song I think; it went to the tune of 'The Carrion Crow' and as fast as 'The British Grenadiers', or faster if you could manage:

The –
*Trous*ers and the petticoat fell down a well, says the
Trousers to the petticoat *I* can't tell –
*What*'ll your mistress do without you, says the
Petticoat in answer I'll tell *you*. She'll
*Cove*r up her rump, she'll cover up her rump, she'll
Get a bit of carpet and cover up her rump. She'll
*Cove*r up her rump, she'll cover up her rump, she'll
*Cove*r-up-her-rump she'll *coverrupperrump*!

When sung by a lot of men, it gives the rousing effect of drums.

Of his own songs 'The Islands' was his favourite and I heard it once at least on every sail with Mr Belloc. When sailing along a lovely coast with a fair breeze in the evening, it was a beautiful accompaniment.

It was a thundery afternoon and the wind played tricks. A dramatic sight as we came past Orford Ness was a so-called 'line squall', an effect produced by a steep wedge of the cold air of a cold front undercutting and lifting the warm air in a depression with unusual rapidity. As it came towards us, the dark rain clouds were literally rolled up before it. The front part of the roll seemed to be tumbling down out of the heavens, as if to fall right on to us – very threatening. Behind this was clear sky and presumably wind to come. We lowered the mains'l in anticipation of some violent gusts, but though a squall did come, with darkened and ruffled sea stretching out from the Ness, it was not very heavy; an anticlimax, in fact. But further out to seaward a water spout was visible, an unusual thing to see in these waters, showing that the surface air as well as the lofty atmosphere was strangely disturbed. We reached Lowestoft in the early morning after a night of calms and uncertain airs and Mr Belloc, still not very well, decided he would leave us here and not sail back to Pin Mill.

In the harbour there were two or three ketch-rigged trawlers still to be seen among many power-driven vessels of all sizes. We were loath to go into the special yacht basin with no motor for manœuvring; instead we were helped to berth alongside a trawler. Personally I have always found whatever the size of the boat or 'yacht' I am in, that fishermen, no matter what the size of their own vessel, are helpful and do not seem to regard you as having no business to be there or as merely a nuisance. There is kindness in what they do and what feels like a sort of respect, but it is more, I think, a show of sympathy for people who, although only amateurs, venture out to sea like them and have to contend with its dangers and hardships.

As he was getting into the dinghy to go ashore, Mr Belloc lost his balance slightly and sat down very heavily on the stern seat. He landed right on the ring bolt, which struck the root of his spine (the coccyx was probably fractured). He gave a yelp and uttered a lot of curses. He had pain on sitting down for weeks afterwards, and when we met him later in the Reform Club he was still uttering elaborate curses over the incident. He felt the vulnerability of his age; still knocking about the sea in a sailing boat in his late sixties.

# ON HAVING NO BRAKES
# AND THE 'BOWSPRIT TRICK'

THERE are only a few things you can do to bring a boat to a standstill when she has way on under sail power. The first is to come up into the wind with the sails flapping till the wind stops her and would blow her backwards if nothing else is done. If the place where she stops is where you want to stop, for instance within grabbing distance of a mooring buoy of suitable size, well and good. But the distance to be allowed for the boat to lose all way requires judgement and knowledge of the performance of that particular vessel. The second is suitable when you are approaching a quay to which you wish to tie up. You let the sheets go and the sails flap empty of wind while you continue on your course tangentially towards the quay. It takes longer to slow down than it does when coming up into the wind, and if the wind is aft of the beam it continues to blow you along a bit and you may be obliged to take the sails down. But if you bungle the approach to the quay and the wind, coming from off the quay, blows you away from it, you may have to hoist the sail again in a hurry and make a fresh approach.

Dropping a kedge anchor over the stern is a third way of stopping abruptly in an emergency, but this seems to be seldom if ever done; who is there who goes about with a kedge and warp perpetually at the ready on the after deck in case of such a crisis?

'Scandalizing' the mains'l, on the other hand, is an excellent way of coming to a halt in a vessel driven by sails alone and is described on page 140 in 'The Veere Canal'.

But there is one more way worth mentioning, which I shall call the 'bowsprit trick'; a method unique to the good ship *Jersey* and practised only once, in Ostend in 1934. This was on a long sail, taking us across the Channel to Dunkirk and Ostend, where Mr Belloc left us, and then on to Flushing and the Veere Canal. The party included Mr Belloc, Roughead, my brother Michael and myself. We had intended to tie up at a certain long quay in one of the docks, as a preliminary berth. A fair wind slightly astern had

Fig. 12. Captain and crew executing the bowsprit trick.

carried us into Ostend and we were still going at a speed of about two knots when the moment came to make the tangential approach to this quay. We had been slow in getting the mains'l down due to some hitch and when close to and parallel to the quay were still going much too fast. Now this dock had a brick wall at its far end, which formed a right-angled corner with the quay in question. Into this corner we were now going with a momentum of 19 tons mass times 2 knots velocity and the imminent certainty of hitting the wall head-on with our bowsprit. The force of the shock might either splinter it or cause it to ram inboard, breaking the bitts or anything in its path, or alternatively knock a great hole in the brick wall, which did not look as if it would stand very much.

I had a sudden thought and, rushing to the foredeck, seized the iron handle of the winch and with it knocked out the great wooden pin that held the bowsprit in place. Then came the impact. Freed from its lateral confines, the square butt end of the 21-foot spar thrust inboard. There was a rope that must have been used as an out-haul, which ran in a groove round the butt end and was cleeted on the bitts. I had undone this at the moment of knocking out the pin and now used it as a means of checking the speed of the backward-travelling sprit. In it came and on the *Jersey* went towards the wall, but slowing all the time. The butt end went past the mast as far as the companion and the ship came quietly to a stop with her stem head a foot from the wall and the bowsprit neatly housed, all 21 feet of it. It was the perfect buffer and had done the trick beautifully. The whole thing from impact to full stop took about seven seconds. Bursting with laughter and triumph we leapt on to the quay and set to at the normal business of berthing with warps and bollards.

### MORAL

In harbours where the authorities do not provide buffers, as they do at railway termini for locomotives that cannot quite slow down in time – improvise your own.

# MR BELLOC IN OSTEND

IN the short cruises of the previous two summers we had felt concern for Mr Belloc's physical sufferings and his complaints about old age but were not particularly worried about him. This year we were. Our cross-Channel venture to Ostend and elsewhere was, after all, a longer sail than usual. He had always groaned or grunted when letting himself down into the dinghy or heaving himself up over the side by the shrouds and yelped when he sat heavily on something uneven, but it took a very hard day to tire him out. He seemed as strong as any of us, although not quite so agile. This year, however, he began to have attacks of giddiness. After we had crossed the Channel and were ashore in the streets of Dunkirk and especially Ostend, he several times wanted to stop or sit down in any chance café and ask for coffee and brandy, or took a swig from his hip-flask instead.

He was maddened by the new noisiness of town life which started in the 1930s with the rise of the automobile and has been in crescendo ever since. The motor bicycle had suddenly become cheap and was being deliberately made a noisy machine to please the young. These things were always roaring round side streets, the quiet streets he liked, making him furious. The back-firing of a motor bike hurt him like a blow on the head. His curses were awful to hear and I thought it would be very bad for his blood pressure that he should be put into a rage so often. I felt I ought to establish the cause of these attacks; but as a hardly fledged young doctor I could only think of cerebral thrombosis and the threat of a stroke. Only a very experienced physician could properly have summed up this unique patient. His heart may have been very sound (indeed he lived for another twenty years), his blood pressure may have been quite reasonable, his liver none the worse for years of drinking wine. He never drank whisky or gin, cocktails or aperitifs or large amounts of beer and once, when asked about his consumption of alcohol, said 'I don't drink alcohol, I drink *wine*'. At any rate, anent the problem of his giddiness, in medical terms both alcohol and caffeine are dilators of blood vessels and therefore his own remedy, brandy and coffee, I thought was probably right, being likely to dilate both the cerebral and the coronary arteries.

After his first attack in Ostend, he walked back to the harbour with shuffling steps (he refused a taxi), got aboard the *Jersey* with many sighs and fell asleep on his rubber mattress. In the evening he revived on food and wine, gradually all his vigour returned and he and all of us were hilarious until midnight. It was on this or a similar occasion, drinking in the cabin of the *Jersey* by the light of a lantern and a few candles, that he talked of his early years in politics and how he had begun one of his election speeches with 'Gentlemen, I am an alien, a Papist and pro-Boer!' It was a fine phrase and after such an opening one can imagine his audience could not but hear him out. It calls for thought.

Mr Belloc was an alien in that he was of French patrilineal descent and of French nationality by birth. He was also a European, or a man with a much greater knowledge of and love for Europe than his audience, so that he was, relatively to their lives, an alien. And yet he was also an Englishman who loved and knew England intimately and was brought up from childhood in Sussex, where his heart remained and his patriotic feelings were rooted.

The word Papist he used fearlessly and provocatively. Although his being a Catholic was at that time an obstacle on many professional roads he might have wished to take, he always insisted on declaring it and loudly making it known that the Catholic faith was far more important to him than the project in hand, the *campagne* or anything else.

As for the Boer War, as a military strategist he admired the courage of the Boers and their tactics and tenacity in defending their farms, and he backed them in the fight. He was totally sceptical as to the alleged motives of those who promoted this war, believing that behind it all was the lure of the South African mines and work of international financiers. The driving of farmers out of their homelands roused his strongest hostility.

His tiredness and his giddiness recurred, however, and between ourselves we began to say 'ought he to go on?' Perhaps our worries were exaggerated. He knew himself better than we did. But one day when I was alone with him, I had an awful moment when I thought Mr Belloc was dying. We had gone ashore without him and he stayed on board to read or sleep. I came back before the others and stepped aboard quietly from the quayside. I sat on the hatch cover for a while inspecting the decks and rigging with my eye. Suddenly I heard a sound like heavy breathing coming from the cabin; it took me a few moments to decide if the sound was human or not. They were long husky hollow sounds, rather like a broken-winded horse but slower. What on earth was happening? In two leaps I was down the hatchway. There was Mr Belloc blowing up his great rubber mattress with his own breath.

'My dear, I'm so glad you've arrived. That little contraption' – pointing to the small concertina-like bellows that was supposed to do the job – 'is no use to man or beast. I'm trying to blow the thing up with my own lungs, which are ten times better than it, even at my age – the valve keeps leaking.'

'Sir, I thought you were dying!' I said, which produced a burst of laughter.

'Well – you might have been *right*, my dear, you might have been *right*!'

It was an old-fashioned characteristic even in those days to carry a lot of money on you. Whereas most people now would carry a chequebook and credit card, when travelling or on a cruise, in the *Jersey* Mr Belloc took with him a thick wad of notes. One did occasionally catch sight of a five or ten pound note of crisp and thin but tough white paper; but what he took out of his breast pocket most often was an oblong wallet containing a solid block of new one pound notes, a good half inch thick. Those old pound notes, worth so much then compared to now, were printed in brown ink and of beautiful design, with an etching of the Houses of Parliament on the back. They were held firmly in place by double-hinged criss-cross elastic bands of ingenious design so that the wallet could be opened in either direction – a thing of endless fascination to me as a child, and even now.

This was not Hilaire Belloc posing as a rich man. The sums he carried in his inner pockets were probably quite small compared with those then carried by 'the rich', whom he envied and also derided. It was Belloc enjoying the safety and the power that money gives to the traveller, or rather gave; for the risk of being attacked and robbed was negligible in those times. I asked him if he had ever lost the wallet. He said only once in many years, and as he put it away he slapped his pocket and said with an ironical gleam in his eye, 'always carry plenty of money on you, my boy'.

Annoyed by Ostend and probably feeling that he was not altogether fit for the sail back to England with the uncertainties of weather and fatigue, Mr Belloc decided to go to Brussels, leaving us to continue north and then sail the *Jersey* home. But first we were all to come along with him for the day and see Brussels, leaving the *Jersey* in the yacht basin to look after herself. There was, after all, nothing inside her or on deck to tempt a thief. At about 9 a.m. the next morning he appeared on deck in full black town clothes – the low-crowned black hat, a light black cloak, polished boots, gold-rimmed pince-nez with black ribbon, black tie, clean white shirt and a large Gladstone bag. Soon we were all bundling into a train. People must have thought it was odd that such a distinguished gentleman, questionably a man of this century, should be accompanied by four young men dressed in shabby trousers and jerseys. Appearances and clothes never mattered to Mr Belloc, if the man himself looked all right; but his own did. He took us to lunch in a large restaurant and ordered Burgundy, saying that the Belgians liked it much more than Bordeaux and that all the best Burgundy in France went to Belgium and Brussels was full of it. Afterwards he showed us the famous Market Square, such an infinitely quieter place in those days. Now, packed with parked cars and jammed with traffic, with flashing signs and displays for the tourist, its dignity has gone and the gold-embossed stone of the tall old houses escapes notice. There we thanked him and said goodbye and wished him well on his next move – to Paris. He had been to a bank and obtained money in Brussels, but I think he could always have gone wherever he wanted on that block of pound notes in his breast pocket.

# OSTEND TO FLUSHING

FROM Ostend we sailed on to Holland. We reached Flushing
and tied up in the Dock from which, through an inner lock,
one enters the Middelburg Canal. This runs north-east to the port
of Veere, our final destination.

It was sad not to have Mr Belloc with us. He would so have
enjoyed this little voyage of discovery, this voyage into the past,
for in the 1930s the islands of the Scheldt were to outward
appearances still in the seventeenth century, and the tempo of life
seemed to be about the same as of that period. The fastest thing
on the road was the bicycle, though there were, of course, cars in
Flushing and one might occasionally meet one in the remoter
parts of the island of Walcheren. In the market place of Middelburg one saw country people with very old styles of clothes and in
the islands of Marken, now joined to the mainland, everyone was
in peasant costume, the Catholics and Protestants being sharply
distinguished from each other by their dress, as two armies would
be by their uniforms.

It was said that such traditions were kept up only for the sake
of tourists. But in those days and even in the late 1940s after the
war and before polderization joined them to the mainland,
the islands of Zeeland were cut off by the swirling high tides
of the estuary of the Rhine or the mud and sand wastes of its low

tides and could be reached only by ferry boats, boyers and botters – rather a difficult journey for most tourists. Some of the women wore the most enormous headdresses of starched white linen, most unsuitable, one would think, for such a windswept place. I saw a little party of them going downwind rather fast and it was obvious that a sort of helmsmanship was required to keep on the path, for to suffer an accidental gybe was to risk losing all! Though Mr Belloc certainly knew parts of Holland well, he did not, I think, know these islands, and the resistance to change that was to be seen there would have delighted him. He was fascinated by the Dutch and wrote masterfully of their towns.

A year or two before this I had been here with Eric Clarke in our little 19-foot Aldeburgh sprat boat and sailed through the Middelburg Canal to Veere, a charming little town and fishing port that looks across the east Scheldt to south Beveland. It is a splendid wide, straight canal with no locks until you get to Veere where there was a sea lock that let you out into the east Scheldt.

The town of Middelburg is half-way and here the canal becomes a sort of inland port, with many barges loading and unloading, which you sail past. After that cruise, I had begun to consider the possibility of doing the same thing in the *Jersey*. A south-west to north-west wind would do, but I was chiefly worried about the width of the canal and the awful possibility of having to tack if the wind veered to the north. The northerly direction of the canal would make it impossible to hold a course in such conditions. Information as to the exact width, of course, could have been obtained by reference to a Dutch almanac, but how does one get hold of such a thing?

In the event, returning in the *Jersey*, I felt my memory was reliable enough and when the day came and we did indeed have to tack we succeeded – but only just. Was it foolish even to think of sailing through the Middelburg Canal in an ancient gaff-rigged boat with no motor and, more important, in common with all sailing craft – no brakes? Perhaps it was, but what a lovely experience it proved to be.

After some time ashore in Flushing, we cast off and made our way to the inner lock that gave access to the canal. The man who controlled the gates asked no questions. He probably assumed we had a motor and that the reason why we hoisted the stays'l, to give us steerageway across the basin with the puffs of wind that came over the roof tops, was either a commendable economy with petrol or because we liked to do it that way – Holland has always been a land of sails and wind. There was a west wind, on our port side; it was a fair wind for Veere. With mainsail hoisted and peak set high we started down the canal at speed. The possibility of doing some damage costing thousands of guilders was pushed to the back of my mind.

# THE VEERE CANAL

THE opening of a lock gate has a magical effect. One is reminded of scenes in operas when great doors in palaces or temples glide apart to reveal something awesome, the God, the High Priest, a conqueror, Valhalla. After you have gone down in a lock and are waiting in a sort of wet dungeon, with the sound of water squirting in fountains from between the closed gates behind you and pouring like a hundred taps from cracks in the walls, suddenly a slit of light appears in the tall barrier ahead. It widens slowly. There is no rush of water inwards or outwards, all is quiet. Very slowly the great doors fold back into the walls. The lock is filled with light. The sky, which had been high above your head in the dungeon, comes down to the new horizon which appears before you. A shining surface of water lies ahead and you glide out on to it to start a new adventure. There is similar magic in going up. As you enter the dungeon the great doors close behind you as if for ever. The splashing noise that fills the air as you enter is then drowned by a great rumbling, whirling and hissing as the water foams and rises. You are lifted up from the pit to find again a new horizon. The gates open outwards to reveal, as after a descent, a bright sheet of water at your own new level. It is yours, it is waiting for you and on to it you glide with new excitement and new hopes.

The canal from Flushing to Veere on the north-east coast of the island of Walcheren is about ten miles long. Middelburg, as the name implies, is about half-way. The direction from Flushing to Middelburg is 10 degrees east of true north; thereafter it runs north-east for three miles and then due north for the last two. A west wind is a fair wind; even north-west might just be sailable

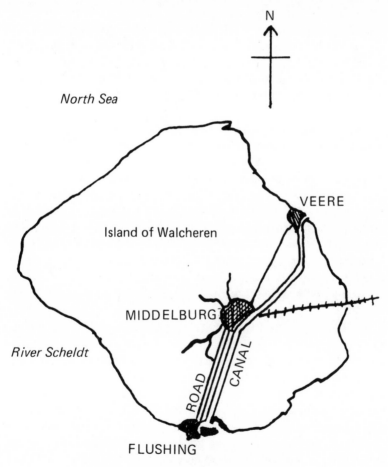

Fig. 13. The canal from Flushing to Veere.

without tacking, so we were pretty confident about getting through to the end. However, there were two bridges between Flushing and Middelburg which might be tricky. These could be raised to allow a boat to pass through, provided the bridge keeper saw you in time. For our part, with no motor, the approach would require some careful sailwork.

As I have said before, it is difficult to stop a sailing boat except by taking the sails down or coming up into the wind, or letting them flap; but you can't do that if the wind is behind you, or on the quarter. A sailing boat is a brakeless means of transport, a brakeless, floating conveyance driven by the wind and questionably suitable for travelling on canals. But after all, the Dutch had been doing it for centuries. Our loose-footed mainsail provided the perfect answer.

The old-fashioned fisherman's manœuvre of 'scandalizing' the mainsail is performed by tricing up the tack (the lower front corner of the sail) by means of a tackle (pulley), as high as the jaws of the gaff (see fig. 14), much as a woman may gather her skirts up her legs to the knee or higher (hence, perhaps, the origin of the term 'scandalize'?). This takes only half a minute to do and the area of sail is reduced by about one-third. The power of the sail can then be further reduced by lowering the peak. When the gaff is horizontal, the sail flaps and billows but does not drive the boat (see fig. 15). If you have slowed down too soon, the peak can be hoisted again for a few minutes or the stays'l raised, whichever you like.

We did not quite know what to expect when the first bridge came in sight. Nor, perhaps, did the bridge keeper when he first caught sight of a large gaff-rigged cutter charging down the canal under full sail. But to our delight it began to open while we were still some way off; one half of it, hinged on the west side, was being raised by a Van Gogh-like structure which operated it. The gap through which we had to pass looked rather small. Although it would have been possible to go through under full sail at about four knots, it seemed rash or at least discourteous to do so. Down jib and stays'l, therefore, followed by a tricing up of the tack and

Fig. 14.

Fig. 15.

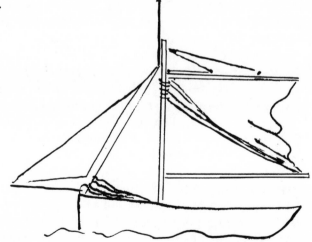

Figs. 14 and 15.  Scandalizing the mainsail.

moderate lowering of the peak. This brought our speed to a stately one knot at the critical moment of passing through. We kept close to the west, the windward side, and brought the boom well in. The gaff did not hit anything. A gratifying queue of carts and bicycles had accumulated on each bank. We tried to look as if this was everyday stuff for us and the friendly nod of the bridge keeper seemed to indicate it was certainly so for him.

The second bridge at Middelburg was equally obedient to the needs of our brakeless floating vehicle, but in fact we wanted to stop and go ashore and see the town first. There appeared to be a pontoon and some pylons to tie up to on our side of the bridge, so while still some way off we tried to indicate to the bridge keeper, by slowing down considerably and leaning out over the port side holding a rope, that we were going to do this. We were understood. The bridge remained shut. We came on. This time we had really got to stop or there would be trouble, but a certain amount of speed was necessary for the ship to respond to the helm. We had a bowline ready to throw over the first pylon. But the pylon was rather tall and when the moment came we missed it. Everyone except me leapt on to the pontoon, more warps were thrown and someone managed to get a turn round a pylon and hang on. With much creaking and straining the *Jersey* was brought to a halt. It was a scramble, but effective. We tied up respectably, with mainsail lowered and everything made shipshape so as to impress the Dutch. We then spent a few hours in the seventeenth century.

The quiet and the charm of Middelburg put you in the atmosphere of a dream or fairy tale. It was a silent town except for the occasional rattle of a cart or barrow over the brick paving or a bicycle bell rounding a corner. The automobile, you could believe, had not yet been invented. Perhaps because it was the middle of the day there was hardly anybody about, but, as if the town were absorbed in its own dream, the sound of a string quartet came from the upper windows of a house. All doors were shut and lace curtains made it hard to discern any human life within, but the occupant of the house could certainly see you. Every house had one or more mirrors attached to the sides of the windows, like the wing mirrors of cars only somewhat larger, and these were placed at such an angle as to reflect your image into the interior as you stood on the doorstep. I experimented by standing near the door of a house in a little side street and looking straight into one of the mirrors. From the dark front room a pair of eyes stared back at me.

Perhaps in the evening the town would wake up a bit, but we had to be off down that canal again. This time we could tell the bridge keeper in advance what we were intending to do, which was to set the mainsail while still tied up to the pontoon, with peak high to catch the breezes coming over the roof tops, and then let go. All went well, with an amused crowd of Dutch folk watching on the bridge head. Nothing to pay.

The next few miles of the canal were in a north-easterly direction and the wind, though veering north-west, was still fair, in fact abeam, and we made great speed. As the last stretch of the canal was due north, however, the boat's windward-sailing capacity was going to be put to the test. The canal looked wide enough for there to be just room for a short tack if necessary, depending on the banks being steep-to. She pointed up the canal well, as if to make Veere in one long tack, but alas there was the leeway to reckon with. At about half-way it was clear we would have to attempt the tack, and if we failed, would then be in for a two-mile tug from the tow path. I bore away slightly to gather speed for the turn into the wind and just as I was about to put the helm over the ship's bows rose in the air and a deep rumble came from the keel. The suddenness and steepness of the rise gave one the impression of being on the back of a large male animal mounting a female and there, in this ridiculous position, we stuck – sails flapping, rudder powerless. So the canal banks were not steep-to! There appeared to be a shelf projecting five yards out from the bank, with only three or four feet of water on it before the true depth of the canal. It was a very hard shelf and the boat did not plunge into it but slid up on to it.

I immediately contrived a manœuvre which I thought might not only get us off, but get her head round at the same time as if we had tacked; and it worked. Two of the heaviest of us stood on the tip of the counter, I held the tiller to port standing with my weight as far back as I could, and a fourth took one of our long oars and thrust with all his strength against the hard shelf. To our delight the *Jersey* slid off backwards. It was rather like the launching of a ship. Then, with reversed helm, the backwards impetus could be used to steer her in a semicircle until her stern was pointing at the bank we had just got off. A backing of the stays'l brought her head round and we were in a position as if we had just successfully tacked. It seemed wise to gather speed by

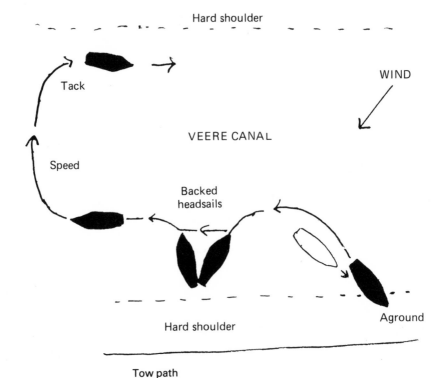

Fig. 16. The *Jersey*'s reversed three-point turn after getting off the bank of the Veere Canal.

Michael MacCarthy, Roughead and D.M. going
ashore in Ostend.

Middelburg, on the Veere Canal, in 1935.

Approaching Harwich the morning after the leak
described in 'A Nightmare in the North Sea'.

The Chapman Light in the Lower Thames as it was in 1939, looking west. Hole
Haven is on the right and Shell Haven beyond it. From a watercolour by D.M.

Mr Belloc and D.M. in pensive mood, but not Roughead.

The *Jersey*'s deck, with D.M. in the companionway, showing some of her heavy tackle.

The *Jersey*'s last resting place, a mud berth at Hole Haven, Canvey Island, depicted by D.M.

Hilaire Belloc aged 79, photographed by Jim Hall in 1949.

running a little way back towards Middelburg, keeping near the leeward bank. We then made a tight turn up into the wind. She came about all right over by the windward bank and on we went. Whether we had to make more than one tack I cannot recall, I think we did, but we got to Veere without running on to the hard shelf again. We tied up to a pontoon for the night, ready to enter the sea lock for the east Scheldt at a suitable time.

Although Veere was hardly more than a fishing village, it did boast a cathedral. This enormous edifice could be seen from miles away. When you got near, it became apparent that it was only the north transept of a cathedral that had either fallen down or had never been completed. Why such a vast church had been planned in this remote place is difficult to imagine. Veere had a little mall surrounding a tiny, drying-out harbour, packed with fishing boats of a very antiquated type. They had inward-leaning slab sides, lee boards, sails and trawls and some had motors. There were ramparts round the seaward (north) side and a little hotel, probably once a customs house, looked down from them upon the fishing fleet and out across the east Scheldt.

Here my friends left to return to their normal occupations and I awaited the arrival of two more whom I went by bus to meet in Flushing; Hubert Howard, whom I did not yet know but whose brothers I knew well, and Kim Norton, an American friend of Hubert's. Kim was an expert on ocean racing, but had been warned that when he stepped aboard he would step into another century. We had a lovely easy passage across the outer Thames Estuary to Harwich with gentle westerly breezes. They did most of the steering and I for once was able to do some cooking. Probably for the first time since the *Jersey* left her Channel Island home, the smell of *pot-au-feu*, but with Dutch onions and vegetables, came floating up the hatchway.

# A NIGHTMARE
# IN THE NORTH SEA

I HAVE several times mentioned the worrying underthought one had when at sea in the *Jersey*, that something might give way when she was hard-pressed, some not visible parts of her frames might be rotted through or that some of her planking might burst open as in the incident with the Hythe lifeboat, to produce a situation that pumps and human strength could not cope with. But when one approached her in the dinghy, riding at anchor, fearless of the sea among a fleet of graceful but delicate-looking yachts, or when standing on her splendid broad decks, it was easy to put such fears behind one.

It was in the late summer of 1938, just before the Munich declaration and several years after our cruise to Holland, that five of us, without Mr Belloc, set out to sail the *Jersey* once more across the southern North Sea; this time from the Belgian fishing harbour of Nieuwpoort to Harwich. I was accompanied by Eric Clarke and two other medical friends, Alec Innes and Hugh Cartwright. Who the fifth was I cannot remember. The length of the passage was about eighty-four land miles (seventy-three nautical miles) and the course north-west. A westerly wind was prevailing and there were no warning signs of worsening weather. We carried no wireless for shipping forecasts. If the conditions did not alter much it would take us about twenty-four hours. We left in the afternoon and were well out in the North Sea, about a third of the way across, by midnight. There was a half moon but it gave little light owing to heavy cloud. The wind blew harder towards midnight, force five or six. We had one reef in. We had to sail the *Jersey* fairly close-hauled to lay the course and the going was uncomfortable – sea moderate to rather rough.

Cartwright and Innes and the fifth man were asleep in their bunks and Eric and I were on watch. I went below for some purpose and was aghast to find the whole cabin awash. The dim light of the hurricane lamp showed the floor covered so deep that the water was sloshing from side to side and making a sound like waves against rocks. It was a repeat of the near sinking episode between Folkestone and Dungeness four years earlier and of our eventual rescue by the Hythe lifeboat. But this time there would be no lifeboat and the nearest place of safety was Harwich, sixty miles to the north-west, or the Belgian ports, thirty miles to the south-east. Ramsgate was fifteen miles away but dead to windward. My heart sank and my solar plexus emitted awful sensations.

We hove her to with backed headsails and tiller tied to leeward. She laid quieter in the sea, which was easier for pumping, but the motion was more up and down and that added nausea to my fear and despair. The only other benefit from a smoother motion was that the rushing of the waves in the cabin became less violent. Now to the pumps. Alec Innes was soon on deck and he and Eric primed the gut-stretcher and were soon throwing out the water. I went below to work the rotary pump. Cartwright and the fifth man were fast asleep. I left them, for the time being; their turn would soon come. Would half an hour's pumping do the trick? Or was she leaking very fast?

After about twenty minutes I could see not the slightest abatement of the flood in the cabin! Waves still slopped against the lockers and over my boots. Solar plexus pangs began again. I went to the hatch and shouted to them to keep at it as we were still not winning. In the next ten minutes or so many things went through my head as I pumped desperately by the dismal light of the swinging lantern and watched the water level to judge if it was rising or falling. We were not five miles from safety as we had been off Folkestone, but thirty. If we were filling rapidly and sank in a few hours what chance would five men have in a 10-foot dinghy, with a fresh breeze and breaking seas? We had no rocket signals to fire but even if we had, in the middle of the North Sea in the dark what a hope! Could we get the internal ballast out of the bilge and up over the side to lighten her – huge slippery iron pigs weighing about 40 kilos each? An appalling job. Would we end with desperate baling with buckets and basins as well as pumping? The flood was *not* abating; that was certain now. We were in a very serious plight. At this rate we should surely sink in a few hours. I was plunged into despair and a childish kind of misery. YACHT FEARED LOST WITH FIVE MEN IN NORTH SEA said an almost hallucinatory voice in my head.

Then there came a shout from on deck. 'There's nothing coming up now – is she dry?' 'No!' I shouted back, 'she's filling.' At the same time there was a strange sucking noise under the floor. My God! I thought, the main pump must be blocked. We must clear it or she'll be done for all the sooner. I tried with my nails to get a floorboard up and see what had happened. Hopeless! The boards, normally quite loose, were jammed tight, swollen with the soaking they had had in sea water. I got my knife out and rammed it between two boards and managed to prise one up. To my amazement the water started to pour away into a black empty space beneath. The bilge was dry! 'Thank God!' I shouted, I don't know how many times. With a few rolls of the ship the sloshing waves vanished under the floor like the last of the bath water going down the plughole. 'She's dry!' I shouted up, 'come and see!' The swollen planks had become watertight and had held the water above the cabin floor, giving the impression that in spite of half an hour's pumping the level was as high as ever. All that was necessary now was to pump out the residue, nearly another bilgeful, but this time with the cheerful certainty that we were winning. No one but me had been subject to this ghastly false impression. I had been alone in my despair and misery; my nightmare. And now I was alone in my relief and thankfulness; though Eric, who had seen the flooded cabin before he went to the pump, and had spent an anxious half hour, having been through the Hythe lifeboat affair and knowing what slavery to the pumps was like, understood my nightmare when I told him.

No one has much sympathy for someone who has had a fright about nothing, and when Cartwright said next morning 'What on earth was going on last night? When I was half awake I heard someone shouting *thank* God!' everyone had a good laugh at this.

But I had learnt something. And I kept it to myself because I was ashamed of it. It was that faced with the near certainty of drowning, after a struggle lasting perhaps many hours, fear had had the most awful physical effects on me: a general weakness, almost paralytic, a jelly-like feeling in the joints, a coldness in the skin and violent screwing of the guts – which did not, however, result in my filling my pants; that at least I am proud to relate. Hope seemed to me to be down to zero: what was there to cling to? The 'can't-happen-to-me' instinct did its best to sustain me, but it was a faint voice in my ear against the hard facts shouting at me, false though they proved to be. As the years have gone by, which included the Second World War, I have gradually learnt to detach myself from these bodily sensations when confronted with the threat of danger. It is a matter of saying to oneself 'These sensations are damnable, but they are only sensations not an illness, not a true incapacity, not a disintegration. My body can work and is working. They are highly unpleasant but to be endured like a pain, for so long, till the danger recedes or is over.' One's reasoning powers can then better prevail.

What dangers or threats am I referring to? Only experiences that many have had, such as (in my case) the start of one of the big London blitzes in 1942; going to 'action stations' in a warship and having to make my way five decks down, closing five watertight doors above me as I went; climbing cliffs alone and getting stuck on a precipitous slope, too scared to go on and too scared to go back; and going up the Mont Cenis Pass in France in a car in snow without chains, getting stuck and slowly skidding backwards nearer and nearer to the fatal edge. On that occasion I felt the blanching of the skin as a physical sensation and saw that my hands were white: an effect of adrenalin. A sudden danger does not have time to call forth these physical side-effects. It is the threat of danger, near or some way off, that does it and the imagination can always exaggerate the threat, or see as a threat what a more experienced person would not be worried by.

There is no denying that when cruising and passage-making by sail one encounters situations fairly frequently that are to some degree threatening. Everyone feels an uncanny lowering of morale in fog, and the combination of fog, fast tides and rocks particularly requires strong nerves. There are some predicaments, chiefly those of heavy weather, the outcome of which is a matter of endurance. Confidence in one's own or other people's stamina may make the prospect simply one of tedium rather than of danger. But seasickness, inexperience and too much imagination may seriously undermine endurance.

In this short episode I had panicked somewhat because I saw in it a replica of a previous experience in the *Jersey*; but with the difference that we were thirty miles from safety instead of five and it was at night. I considered the endurance factor very seriously while I was pumping, as being the only hope, but thought the strength required was probably beyond our capacity. I would have been proud if the story had afterwards been told by someone as follows:

Getting everyone on deck he put it to them that it was only a matter of time before the boat would sink. They could not beat the leak with the two pumps, they could only delay the end. Harwich was sixty miles to go. Ostend was thirty miles downwind. If they kept at the pumps, he said, non-stop, in half-hour shifts for ten to twelve hours and ran for the Belgian coast they might just make it or come across help on the way. As a last resort there were three things they could do to lighten her: get up most of the internal ballast, a very heavy job, jettison the anchor and chain, and get the mainsail off with gaff and boom and tow it alongside. They could have three men on the pumps in a rota of half-hour shifts, one to steer and one to make soup and rig up a distress signal (two black balls or anything resembling two black balls, according to the almanac). No question of all five getting into that dinghy unless they were practically under the water! With a bit of luck and hard work, he said, they ought just to make it. At day-break, however, a Dutch coaster from Groningen passed near enough to recognize the two shirts flying from the masthead as a distress signal and came over. The decks were nearly awash, and they were struggling to get the mainsail and boom overboard. The five men were taken on board and the *Jersey* left to sink, still some twenty miles out from Ostend.

But it did *not* continue like that. Instead of being put to the test I was let off after a brief private view of myself under the influence of despair and adrenalin.

# HOLE HAVEN
# AND HIBERNATION

WE arrived at Harwich in the afternoon, still on the port tack, and the west wind held fair right up the River Orwell, where the green-black September trees and stubble fields came down to the tidal edge. From there the *Jersey* would be taken to her now familiar home at Pin Mill. After the Munich declaration we knew there would be an end to sailing. War was bound to come the next year; we could not plan. Mr Belloc would have liked to have the *Jersey* at Shoreham, but her leaking was such that floating in the dock she would sink, unless pumped out by a man daily, week after week. This would exasperate the Old Man who had already had enough expense to detract somewhat from the joy and pride he first had in the boat. So a mud berth was the thing to find for her. As there was no suitable mud berth to be had at Shoreham, apparently, and as the passage round the South Foreland and down Channel was too long and time-consuming for any of us to undertake at that time, I suggested Hole Haven at Canvey Island near the mouth of the Thames, as a good half-way house in view of the uncertainty of everything. I knew it from previous sailing explorations and had met a local man who would berth her for us.

## PIN MILL TO CANVEY ISLAND

With luck one can have wonderful sailing in October. It was in mid October, about a month after the nightmare in the North Sea, that we made this last passage in the old *Jersey*, alas without Mr Belloc who thought it too late in the year for him. We were four: Eric Clarke, Alec Innes, Hugh Cartwright and myself. We hoped to do it 'on one tide', if the wind was fair; that is, spend the ebb or north-going tide sailing out to the region of the Sunk Head, some fourteen miles south-east from Harwich. Then catch the flood or south-west-going tide and ride on its back all the way up into the Thames. High water at Tilbury is almost two hours later than at the Sunk, so one can have about eight hours of fair tide, though in the first and last hours the current is only weak.

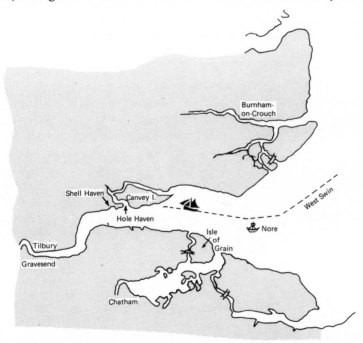

Fig. 17. The *Jersey*'s last passage, Harwich to Hole Haven in the Thames Estuary, in October 1938.

There was a full moon and therefore a spring tide, and to add to our good luck an east wind had set in.

Night passages tend to stick in one's memory. This was the best I ever remember, not only in the *Jersey* but in any boat I have ever sailed. We reached the Sunk Head about midnight and a cold hard wind on our port quarter sent us bowling up the Swin. The sky was swept of all clouds and a blazing white moon put out the stars, all but the brightest of them, as the sun puts them out in the daytime. We rushed along with foaming bows and a hissing wake. And by the way, we pumped dry every two hours.

From the Swin we ran on into the Barrow Deep, from the Barrow Deep to the Oaze, then to the Nore Lightship, on into Sea Reach, the wide River Thames, and at about 9 a.m. passed the Chapman Light, which marks the entrance to Hole Haven. The whole run from the Sunk Head to the Chapman Light is about forty-five sea miles. If we give the tide credit for carrying us ten miles, then we had done thirty-five miles through the water in nine hours, making an average speed of about four knots. Towards morning the wind lessened and our speed dropped, but from midnight through the period of the middle watch we were going at about six knots at times.

It would have been cold for Mr Belloc. If he had been able to come the cabin could have been warmed by a constantly burning primus, or, if he had spent the night on deck in the moonlight, as he might well have chosen to do, he could perhaps have kept warm in the dinghy on deck, with rugs under him and over him. But it was a lot to expect of a man of sixty-eight. It is sad that he was not there on the last sail of the *Jersey*, which might have been the finest of a lifetime even for him.

## THE LONG HIBERNATION

The man in Hole Haven seemed a reliable, old-fashioned type. He prepared a mud berth well up the creek, where the ship would be afloat only at spring tides and so would leak out in the neaps what she took in at springs, thus presenting no pumping problem.

Once, in the early summer of the following year, the *Jersey*, like a hibernating animal emerging to find the sun, did come out for a brief sail, but without Mr Belloc. My three companions were Igor Anrep, Michael Hemans, a young obstetrician, and Douglas Gairdner, a doctor working at the children's hospital at Great Ormond Street, where I was also. He was later to become, in his sixties, one of those enterprising, competent, bold small boat sailors I have mentioned; cruising to the Baltic, to Spain, to Norway, round Ireland and circumnavigating the two halves of the North of Scotland, in a thirty-one footer. Igor Anrep, son of the mosaic artist Boris Anrep, was a medical student, intending at that time to be a psychoanalyst but eventually to become a cardiologist.

Our sail was disappointing. There was no wind. We drifted on the tidal Thames down to the Medway, anchored for the night off the Isle of Grain and returned next day on the tidal Thames again with the faintest puffs of wind. Back in Hole Haven a curious thing happened, characteristic of the hidden treacheries of the old vessel. We had just anchored and the mainsail was still up, but motionless in the calm. Igor, who up till now had not appeared to be enjoying himself one bit, was sitting on the skylight roof in a disconsolate posture. The boom suddenly broke near its outer end, which was supported by the topping lift, and the rest of it came down on his head – a heavy 15-foot spar. Igor said, rather loudly, 'Oh!' and remained sitting and silent. That was the only thing he uttered; but it expressed much. That 'Oh' seemed to say in one breath 'What a boring trip this is! How bloody these doctors are with their endless talk and their silly jokes! What an awful old boat this is! I want to go home.' He did not seem much hurt. He had a slight headache, but was certainly not concussed. After lying down for a while, he asked to be put ashore and he did go home. Looking back on it we ought not to have let him go by himself; but there it is. A blow on the head is enraging and always feels like an insult. He must have felt outraged, but being a man of the most amiable nature he never showed any resentment at the time or when reminded of it in later years.

The *Jersey* went back into hibernation in her mud berth. The man from Hole Haven was paid a lump sum to take the sails off her and store them in his shed along with mattresses and any stealable things such as the dinghy, the anchor, the chain and those beautiful navigation lights. He was then to shut her up, keep a distant eye on her and leave her to the wind and rain. It was for the duration of the war.

When the Dunkirk retreat came and every floating craft that was sound enough put out to rescue whom they could, we – that is Roughead, Jim Hall, Eric Clarke and I – excitedly rang each other up. Should we ask the Old Man if we could take the *Jersey* out again and over to the beaches? We did not do so; but we quite seriously discussed it and what it would really involve. The chief objection was, of course, that she had no motor and during the windless days and nights of that crisis would have been a sitting duck for fighter or bomber aircraft. One could imagine the feelings of soldiers swimming out to this boat and finding they still could not get away. When it was over, all sorts of after-thoughts came to our minds. We could have borrowed an outboard motor for the dinghy and towed the *Jersey* away from the coast as soon as we had taken on board ten or twelve men. But she might have been sunk; we tended to forget that; and she was, after all, Mr Belloc's boat.

# THE LAST DAYS
# OF THE *JERSEY*

THROUGHOUT the war years I had no opportunity to go and see the *Jersey* in her mud berth on Canvey Island, but in 1946 I had a letter from the man at Hole Haven to say that two men from the RAF had been to have a look at her and were interested in buying her. I was demobilized and free, so, acting for Mr Belloc, I went to Canvey Island to meet them and set eyes again on the old *Jersey*. A meeting was arranged at Hole Haven at a suitable state of the tide. I liked the two young men. The *Jersey* had captured their imaginations. They hoped, at best, to be able to repair her and even sail her or at the least to make her into a houseboat. A boat was available which we would row up the creek on the flooding tide to where she lay, right out on a mud island covered by sea lavender, looking across to the old port of Shell Haven.

It was an afternoon of thunder clouds and dramatic skies. There she was, very black against the silvery water of the flood tide and the white westward sky, torn open by a squall. A pair of crows had built a nest at the crosstrees and were circling round and round. How curious to see the origin of the expression 'the crow's nest' for this part of the anatomy of a ship's rigging, illustrated on this old abandoned boat. Perhaps crows in the past have always been on the look out for derelict ships on which to build their nests at the crosstrees, and the *Jersey* was a lucky find for this pair. I made a sketch as we approached and later turned it into a picture. The noble shape of her black hull, though down by the bows and lifted at the stern, rather as if running before a wave, still expressed that grand seaworthy capability. It may well have started ideas in these young men of one day getting her out on the salt again, as Hilaire Belloc would have said.

The planking had burst away from the stern head on the starboard side above and below the water line, and through this breach a foot or so wide the mud-laden sea water flowed in and out on every spring tide. The cabin was full of mud. The airmen thought that if they began by getting all the mud out, then all the pig-iron ballast and then patched over the breach in the bows, she would float out of her berth and could be towed down to a hard somewhere for effective repairs to be attempted. Mr Belloc, now aged seventy-six, thought it a courageous plan and decided to let these commendable young men have the *Jersey*, for a reasonable sum (I do not remember what they proposed), rather than let her lie there for all time, slowly rotting into the mud. So he let her go. Who among the ex-members of the crew had the money to spend and the energy to spare for this big task? We had the love, perhaps, but not the time, being so preoccupied with getting on with life after the war.

I failed to keep in touch with her new owners; perhaps because I did not want to know what really became of the *Jersey*. The possibility of her being made safe for the sea again seemed remote. I think Mr Belloc heard no more. He had wished them well.

# TOO OLD FOR IT

G ROWING old is a painful and slow process, as everyone finds out. If Hilaire Belloc protested more about it than others, it is because to come down from the heights of his physical and mental vigour to the flat plain of the last years of his life was for him a steeper and rougher descent than it is for most men. He destested it; like 'Jim'.

When he was seventy-seven, he and I met at the house of Lady Phipps, who had given him the *Jersey*. He was full of protests about Cardinal Newman's poem 'The Dream of Gerontius'. Old age, he said, was not like that. 'It takes you completely by surprise and springs on you like a tiger, leaving you helpless, in a Bath chair, with two nurses – if you can afford it.' And he summed it up in one word, when asked by Lady Pansy Lamb what getting old was like: 'stinking!'

I did not see him again before he died in 1953, aged eighty-three. He was photographed by Jim Hall at the age of seventy-nine; a sad figure, standing in wait for the click of the camera, lost in thought or perhaps vacancy, with pipe ash down his waistcoat and candle wax on his coat from hours of reading by candles and lighting his pipe from the flame. But these memoirs do not follow him into late old age and death at King's Land. Better a quota-tion, which foreshadows his own last days, from his 'Heroic

Poem in Praise of Wine', written in his late sixties and dedicated to Duff Cooper:

> When from the waste of such long labour done
> I too must leave the grape-ennobling sun
> And like a vineyard worker take my way
> Down the long shadows of declining day.
> Bend on the sombre plain my clouded sight
> And leave the mountain to the advancing night
> Come to the term of all that was mine own
> With nothingness before me and alone –

He was not alone, of course, but lonely as everyone becomes who outlives his oldest friends – lonely as the rock, Old Harry, left out in the sea by the retreating cliffs of Purbeck.

The impressions that remain strongest from those days of Mr Belloc's return to sailing are of his generosity and humanity and the glorious flow of ironic wit. This seems to have been a lifelong form of protest at human failings, his own included, and the despair he felt about it. Laughter was his cure. These sketches are not a study of his character, but may perhaps convey how lovable he was and how proud we were to sail into a port with him; that startling black-clad figure on the deck who took everyone by surprise; that imposing and rather forbidding exterior – so sensitive and kind within.

# APPENDIX
# A BIOGRAPHICAL SKETCH OF
# HILAIRE BELLOC

HILAIRE Belloc was a 'character' on the political and literary stage of the Edwardian period and remained a considerable public figure through the first half of the twentieth century. He was a prolific writer of history, biography, criticism, essays, novels, politics, epigrams, serious poetry, biting satire in light verse and the famous *Bad Child's Book of Beasts* and *Cautionary Tales for Children.* He was a powerful apologist of Roman Catholicism, of the Catholic point of view and of the importance, in interpreting history, of understanding the significance of the decline of the Catholic faith in England.

He was born in 1870 at La Celle Saint Cloud, near Paris, and died in 1953 at his home, King's Land, in Sussex, having lived all his life in England. His father, Louis Belloc, was French, a lawyer. His mother, Bessie Parkes, was English. She was the daughter of Joseph Parkes, a solicitor and a prominent Liberal in his day; one of the founders of the Reform Club. The Belloc family came from Nantes. Hilaire Belloc's grandfather, also named Hilaire, was a portrait painter. He married Louise Swanton, the intelligent and charming daughter of an Irishman, Colonel Swanton, who had fought in Napoleon's campaigns. The Hilaire Belloc of English literary fame was therefore of French, English and a quarter Irish blood.

He had characteristics, both physical and intellectual, which could be considered typically French: stature medium, not tall (5 feet 8 inches, according to an old passport); skull, round; build, square – becoming barrel-chested and *ventru* (large-bellied) in middle age; jaw, wide and square; temperament rational, combative, dominant; and, as an attribute more French than any, an extraordinary fluency and ease of self-expression. These features and the additional oddity of pronouncing his Rs in the French manner, though with a perfect English and not a French accent, produced an aura of the foreigner about him, which some people felt more than others. But it was only a part of his extraordinary personality and presence; an effect produced by his intensely ironical humour, brilliant talk, self-confidence, aggressiveness sometimes – but more often kindness and an old-fashioned courtesy, his husky voice, his black clothes and other eccentricities.

Belloc was brought up in England with visits to France in childhood and adolescence, and educated at the Oratory School (then at Birmingham) where he was strongly influenced by Cardinal Manning, through whom his mother had turned to Roman Catholicism. At the age of seventeen he took British nationality, being already certain that it was in the English language, rather than the French, that his gifts for writing could be more fully expressed. But he did Military Service in France, in the Artillery, an episode which made a deep impression on him. At the rather late age of twenty-two he went to Balliol College, Oxford. While there he became President of the Union and his eloquence and powers of debate in that Society are not forgotten. He took a first-class honours degree in history.

Belloc had great mental energy and also physical energy and stamina. He travelled and tramped for miles, all his active life, in England and parts of Europe he loved. He even walked and hitched the whole way across North America to propose to his future wife, Elodie Hogan. She was of an Irish–American family, living in California. A year later, in 1896, they married and he brought her to England. She bore him five children. Seventeen years later he was to be shattered by her death at the age of only thirty-eight. He wore black and continued certain mourning rituals for the rest of his life.

In 1906 he acquired, as a family home, a rambling house in the Sussex Weald, called King's Land, near Horsham. With it was some land, a few fields that could be farmed and a windmill. The mill was a fine specimen; it has been carefully preserved and to this day can still grind corn. King's Land must have satisfied in him what he felt and always declared was a universal need of man, a necessity in fact, to be the owner of a small or moderate amount of property of some sort. It was at King's Land that he spent the last ten years of his life, cared for by a daughter and son-in-law, cursing the progressive feebleness of body and memory that old age inflicts, and died aged eighty-three.

Hilaire Belloc, who had many ideas of political and economic reform in his head, had a brief episode of political life as Liberal Member of Parliament for South Salford, Lancashire, from 1906 to 1910. He did not achieve reforms or anything that gave him satisfaction. He encountered some corruption, as no doubt he expected to do, and made much of it. He did not stand again and left Parliament in some disillusion, turning to journalism as a better means of influencing public opinion. Politicians became an object of satire for the rest of his life. He hated capitalism and distrusted socialism. He was also anti-imperialist. The fate of Lord Lundy and that of Commander Sin and Captain Blood in *The Modern Traveller* (1898) are two out of many satires in verse that illustrate his antipathies. The often-quoted lines:

> Whatever happens we have got
> The Maxim gun and they have not

were muttered by Captain Blood in this narrative. He stated his views on economics some years later in a book *The Servile State*. About this time, just before the First World War, G. K. Chesterton became a close friend. His journal, *GK's Weekly*, was a successful paper and in it the political creed which Belloc, Chesterton and others shared, known as 'distributism', was put forward. Belloc did an enormous amount of lecturing in England and America, some on politics, but chiefly on history and literature, which meant much travelling and was a strain on his family life. It was also exhausting and a hard way of earning money, but he continued it until he was nearly seventy.

Hilaire Belloc's reputation and popularity as a writer rose high when he became a reporter and commentator on the First World War. He wrote in the weekly journal *Land and Water*, which devoted itself entirely to the conduct and progress of the war and acquired an enormous circulation. Having walked over every mile of the Ardennes and most of Northern France, and having studied military history intensely and served in the French Artillery, he could write with vividness and authority. Incidentally this was the only period of Belloc's life in which he was paid substantially and he became, temporarily, well off.

When, twenty-five years later, the Second World War began he was again in demand as a commentator. But this time his success was short-lived, for although he knew the terrain as well as ever, the conduct of war had so utterly changed, with new weapons and tactics, that he was no longer capable of forecasting or explaining things, and – as he put it himself – got the sack.

All his life Hilaire Belloc expressed his many antipathies in his writing and lectures and in doing so often aroused people's antipathy to himself. One of the worst charges against him was his anti-semitism. This was not racial hatred like that of the Nazis, but rather an obsession about the exclusiveness, secretiveness, as he saw it, and financial power of the Jews, which he seems to have imagined to be much greater than it was. He saw that there was a problem concerning them which no one would discuss. And he warned that there would be serious trouble ahead if it was not discussed. Since the pogroms of the Second World War any kind of anti-semitism is unforgivable and the odium of Belloc's intense prejudice, which gave great offence, still sticks to him.

My father, Desmond MacCarthy, said of him in the *New Statesman* (6 June 1925): 'He had an obsession about the ubiquity of financial conspiracies and the degree to which party politics was riddled with jobbery and corruption.' He went on to say: 'Mr Belloc was born with the silver spoon of laughter and that is the mirror he holds up to society.'

So much for politics and journalism; it is on his contribution to history, biography and literature that the fame of Hilaire Belloc rests. It is important that history should be written by fine writers. Ordinary literate or literary people wish to have the past brought alive to them and to feel, when reading history, that they are back in the epoch described. This Belloc could do for them; for he had an astonishing ability to grasp the feelings of our ancestors and what is expressed by their remains, their buildings, portraits, surviving customs and the records of their strifes. It inspired him to write. The clarity and vigour of his prose is impressive; it is also a delight. His biography of Marie Antoinette, published in 1910, is one of the best examples of such writing and considered a great contribution to the history of the French Revolutionary period. Other admired biographies are of Danton (a character that Belloc rather resembled himself), Robespierre, Richelieu, Wolsey, Cranmer, Milton, to mention not even half of them – serious books and profound. He was criticized, perhaps, by academic historians, for his Catholic bias above all; but where is the historian worth reading who has no bias? Belloc said, on the subject of the historian, 'History is not sound because it is readable. But history which is not readable is not history at all.' A fair retort. He also knew full well the errors that lead to falling from history into fiction, but he avoided them.

Many people admire him most as a poet. He had, of course, a marvellous facility with rhyme and metre, as displayed in his satirical verse and pungent epigrams; still remembered and often quoted. But most of his poetry is serious, lyrical, romantic and sometimes touched with genius.

Two of Belloc's books are still well known by name, *The Path to Rome* and *The Cruise of the Nona*. The latter is still in print. The 'pilgrimage' to Rome, though it was not exactly that, was undertaken at the age of twenty, starting from Toul in northern

France. During this long walk his philosophy of life and his Catholic faith crystallized. During that cruise in his sailing boat, the *Nona*, undertaken during the early months after his bereavement in 1914, he writes of the sea with his extraordinary imaginative powers, but the bulk of the book consists of digressions on history that the passing scene evoked and reflexions on the lives of men, as he contemplated the land.

Though he hammered away, his whole life, at expressing the Catholic point of view, and wrote much besides that was extremely serious, Belloc spent most of the time, otherwise, in laughter. When he wrote to amuse, to have fun, to demolish with irony, he was startlingly, explosively funny. So was his conversation; his friends rocked, his audience rocked. He loved wine and drank a great deal of it, also of port and brandy. He shipped wine in cask from France and bottled it at King's Land. He loved good food and knew a great deal about how it should be cooked and served. And he loved staying in the large country houses of some of his friends; his 'rich friends' as he used to call them.

The enormous energy with which Hilaire Belloc was endowed was as much of a curse to him as an asset, causing in him a consuming restlessness. One could hardly think of more suitable advice for someone with a restless nature like Belloc's than for him to go out to sea in a boat that he must handle alone. This was indeed a prescription he made for himself, occasionally. It is extraordinary that he was not drawn or driven by restlessness to spend more time at it. The sailing he did find time for called forth some of his best writing, mostly in the form of essays. These are collected in *Hills and the Sea*, *On Sailing the Sea* and *The Silence of the Sea*.

# GLOSSARY OF NAUTICAL TERMS

ABACK  Said of a sail when the wind catches it on the opposite side to that of its working purpose. Applicable mostly to jibs and foresails.

BACK  To 'back' the headsails is to haul them to the weather side to act as a break to progress and to blow the boat's head round, instead of pulling in the normal way.

BACKSCEND  The confused sea caused by waves deflected from a rocky cliff or mole, which disturbs the motion of a ship. (Sometimes spelt backsend.) *See* Scend.

BILGE  The space between the floorboards of a yacht, or the lowest deck of a ship, and the keel. Also the water in this compartment, usually derived from leakage.

BINNACLE  A fixed box or stand for holding the ship's compass so that it can be clearly seen by the helmsman by day, or by night when it is illuminated from within.

BITTS  Strong posts on the deck of a ship round which ropes can be fastened for towing or mooring.

BLOCK  A wooden or steel case which holds the wheels or sheaves of a pulley. *See* Tackle.

BOWSPRIT  A spar projecting forwards from the bows of a ship, on which the lower end of the jib is set.

BULWARKS  The wooden protecting wall round the upper deck of a ship. In yachts lifelines are usually fitted instead or in addition.

CAPSTAN  A drum, with concave sides, revolving on a vertical axis, fixed to the deck and open at the top so that several turns of rope or cable can be thrown round it. The capstan used to be turned by sailors, each thrusting a pole into the top of the hub as a lever, but a crank handle and cogwheel-drive is fitted to capstans of small vessels.

CAULK  To plug the seam between two planks of a ship's deck or sides with oakum (tow) and seal it over with pitch.

CHAIN-PLATES  Horizontal projections from the ship's sides abreast of the mast, to widen the spread of the shrouds which support it. The whole apparatus of plate, chains and dead-eyes is often referred to as 'the chains'.

COMPANION  Steps or a ladder leading from deck to cabin or saloon, through a framed opening, usually covered by a small deckhouse or hood.

CLOSE HAULED  With all sheets drawn in tightly and the vessel pointing into the wind at the smallest angle possible without the sails flapping; 45 degrees for most yachts or better for some.

COUNTER  An elongation of the after end of the hull or body of a boat, above the water line and aft of the sternpost, thus making a useful extension of the deck for handling sails and other purposes.

DEAD-EYES  A pair of round wooden blocks bored with holes, through which tarred rope passes from block to block in the manner of a pulley. The dead-eyes connect the lower ends of the shrouds with the chains, which are bolted to the ship's sides. Tightening and fastening the tarred rope brings the shroud to the correct tautness.

DRAUGHT  The depth of water between the surface and the lowest point of the keel of a vessel.

FATHOM  The unit by which depth of water at sea or in tidal waters was traditionally measured; 1 fathom = 6 feet.

FLUSH DECK  A deck that is an uninterrupted plane from bows to stern, except for mast, companion and skylights.

FLUKE  The sharp spade-like point of the anchor that digs into the sea bottom.

FO'C'S'LE  Short for forecastle; derived from the ships of the fifteenth and sixteenth centuries, but still applied to the living space in the bows of sailing vessels. Usually called the forepeak in yachts.

GAFF  The wooden spar which supports the upper part of the mainsail. *See* fig. 3, page 33.

GIMBALS  Metal rings within rings, holding the compass or, it may be, a primus stove. The rings are suspended at their fore-and-aft or lateral axes so that the compass in the centre is not affected by the pitch or roll of the ship.

GRAPNELL  A three-pronged hook, to which a rope is fastened, which may be thrown to grab a hold on another vessel for securing or boarding it.

GYBE  The manœuvre of changing the mainsail from one side of the boat to the other when the wind is blowing from behind. If the boom is firmly held amidships at the moment of change-over it is safe, but when a gybe occurs unintentionally with a wide swinging of the boom, damage may be done, especially by a gaff sail when the wind is strong. It is also a danger to any sailor standing on deck and dreaming or deaf.

HATCH  An opening in the deck, usually square, with a removable close-fitting cover or hinged lid.

HELM  The means by which the rudder, and hence the direction of a vessel, is controlled. In small sailing boats and yachts a wooden bar is used, called a tiller. In larger yachts, motor boats and ships, a wheel with various gearing mechanisms replaces the tiller. Both tiller and wheel are referred to as the 'helm'. The man steering is the 'helmsman' and instructions to him may be such as 'Port your helm' or 'Helm-a-starboard'.

JAWS  A two-pronged projection from the lower end of the gaff which grips the mast, though not tightly.

JIB  The foremost of the sails of a cutter, set on the bowsprit and, because of its leverage, exercising a balancing effect on the power of the mainsail. *See* fig. 3, page 33.

KNOT  A speed through the water of one nautical mile per hour. The nautical or sea mile is 2,025 yards (a land mile is 1,760 yards). A boat sailing at six knots is going at about seven miles an hour.

LEE  The side sheltered from the wind. A vessel under sail, unless the wind is directly aft, always has a lee side and a weather side, the side on which the wind is blowing; hence 'windward' and 'leeward' (pronounced 'loo'ard').

LEEWAY  The sideways drift of a vessel in its course, due to the pressure of the wind on sails and hull except when the vessel is running before the wind.

LEE-O!  The helmsman's warning to the crew that he is putting the tiller over to the lee side, which will turn the head of the boat up into the wind, preparatory to going about.

MOLE  A stone jetty or curved wall enclosing a harbour.

PARREL BALLS  Wooden balls, bored like beads, which are threaded on to a cord and strung between the jaws of the gaff. This necklace, as it were, round the front of the mast keeps the gaff from blowing away from it and the jaws from becoming dislocated.

PAWL  *See* Ratchet and Pawl.

PEAK  The upper and outer corner of a gaff mainsail.

PORT and STARBOARD  The port side of a vessel is its left side, to an observer looking from the stern to the bows. Starboard is the right side. Vessels approaching head-on keep to starboard, as we would say 'keep to the right' on land. Orders to helmsmen may be 'port your helm', 'hard a-starboard', etc. The navigation lights of a ship are red for port, green for starboard. For those who can never remember which is which, the tag 'the gentlemen were left with their port' is useful.

PURCHASE  A pulley, also called a tackle, consisting of two blocks with one, two or three wheels to give additional power in setting sails taut.

RATCHET and PAWL  A mechanism of checking the recoil of the drum of a windlass or winch, similar to that of a watchspring. Lifting the pawl allows the drum of a winch or capstan to unwind.

RAT-LINES  Horizontal ropes fastened to the shrouds to make a rope-ladder for ascending to the masthead.

REEF  To reduce the area of a sail. This is done with a gaff or Bermuda sail by bringing it lower down the mast, refastening its inner and outer edges, and tying up the redundant lower part of the sail by means of reef points (cords sewn into the sail for the purpose).

RIDING LIGHT  A white light hung above the foredeck of a vessel at anchor, at night. Obligatory when close to a fairway.

RUNNERS  Additional stays for the mast aft of the shrouds, which can be slackened or tightened by means of a halyard and purchase.

SCEND  The momentum in a wave imparted to a vessel, lifting it or throwing it backwards, sideways or forwards. *See* Backscend.

SCUPPER  The narrow space between the bulwarks and the deck through which sea water or any other water on the deck may run off.

SHACKLE  A U-shaped metal connecting link, with a straight 'pin' closing the U. The pin has an eye at one end and a short screw at the other. Unscrewing the pin allows the insertion of the link of a chain or the eye of some other fitting, a block, a ring bolt, etc. The screw is apt to get jammed unless regularly greased.

SHEAVE  The wheel in the interior of a block over which the rope runs.

SHEET  This is *not* a sail, but the rope which controls a sail, for example a mainsheet or jibsheet. As a large mains'l may exert a very strong pull its sheet is usually run through two or more blocks, one on the boom and one on deck, or a more elaborate system.

SHEER  The rise in the height of the bows and of the stern of a ship from amidships as viewed in profile from a little distance or in the designer's plan. A ship with a deck parallel to the water line has no sheer. A ship whose height above the water line is higher amidships than at the ends, has 'reversed sheer' or is 'hog-backed'. The beauty of the lines of a ship lies often in the sheer, sometimes even in a reversed sheer.

SHROUDS  The main lateral supports of the mast of a yacht, the standing rigging, consisting of strong wires, one or two to each side, looped over the mast at a suitable height and terminating in metal plates, bolted to the ship's planking abreast and just aft of the mast.

STARBOARD  *See* Port.

STAY(S)  Wire supports for fixed spars, the mast, topmast, bowsprit or others. They are called the permanent rigging.

'STAYS'  To 'miss stays' is to fail to come about when tacking. To be 'in stays' is the position of a boat when head to wind and unable to come about or return to the previous tack.

TACK (*n.*)  The lower, forward corner of a gaff mainsail, which is pulled down taut by a purchase after the sail is hoisted.

TACK (*v.*)  To proceed against the wind by making a zigzag course, with sails close hauled, bringing the wind alternately on one side and the other.

TACKLE  Typically a two-block pulley with a hook on one block and a shackle on the other; useful in lifting or pulling anything requiring extra strength. Also called a 'handy Billy'.

TILLER  The wooden (sometimes metal) arm or bar by which the axis of the rudder is rotated and the ship steered when under way.

TOPPING-LIFT  The rope which controls the height of the outer end of the boom. It passes up to the masthead and down to deck level, where it is secured. It takes the full weight of the boom when the mains'l is not set.

TRANSOM  The wide transverse board that forms the box-like stern of dinghies, small yachts and a few larger vessels. This form of construction enlarges the capacity of the interior of the boat and increases the buoyancy of the stern.

TRICE (UP)  To tie up a part or gather up the lower part of a sail so as to reduce its area or see under it.

TUMBLE-HOME  An expression denoting that the sides of a ship above the water line, the 'top-sides', lean inwards so that the width of the upper deck is less than the width of the deck at water level. In section the lines of ships or smaller vessels are generally like those of a wine glass, a cup or a bowl. The ship with 'tumble-home' has a section like a brandy glass.

The advantage of this construction, which is now a thing of the past, is that when the ship heels to the wind the lee topside becomes vertical to the water. Therefore heavy things on the outer edge of the deck, particularly cannon, do not exert so much leverage as they would if the deck were wider. Instead they assert their weight nearer the central pivot of the keel. Also, cannon so placed can still fire.

Some degree of tumble-home was often to be seen in the design of small sailing vessels of the past and even today may add some advantage to the design of a yacht, and has a certain chic.

WEATHER HELM  An expression denoting that a boat has a strong tendency to turn up into the wind when sailing. To correct this the rudder must be used, which requires the 'helm' or tiller to be pulled to the windward or 'weather' side, hence 'weather helm' as a nautical term. Some weather helm is normal and necessary, but a big gaff sail sometimes takes a very strong pull to counteract its turning force.